To:

IS THERE TIME

*Slow Down
Be still, and know
that I am God;
Psalm 46:10a*

David J. Whicker

DAVID J. WHICKER

ISBN 979-8-88943-136-7 (paperback)
ISBN 979-8-88943-360-6 (hardcover)
ISBN 979-8-88943-137-4 (digital)

Copyright © 2023 by David J. Whicker

All rights reserved. No part of this publication may be reproduced, distributed, or transmitted in any form or by any means, including photocopying, recording, or other electronic or mechanical methods without the prior written permission of the publisher. For permission requests, solicit the publisher via the address below.

Christian Faith Publishing
832 Park Avenue
Meadville, PA 16335
www.christianfaithpublishing.com

Printed in the United States of America

ABBREVIATIONS IN THE BOOK

	Abbreviation		Abbreviation
NKJV	New King James Version	KJV	King James Version
NIV	New International Version	LB	Living Bible
MLB	Modern Language Bible	RSV	Revised Standard Version
Gen.	Genesis	Exod.	Exodus
Lev.	Leviticus	Ps.	Psalms
Prov.	Proverbs	Isa.	Isaiah
Jer.	Jeremiah	Dan.	Daniel
Zech.	Zechariah	Matt.	Matthew
Rom.	Romans	1 Cor.	1 Corinthians
2 Cor.	2 Corinthians	Gal.	Galatians
Eph.	Ephesians	Phil.	Philippians
1 Thess.	1 Thessalonians	2 Tim.	2 Timothy
Heb.	Hebrews	1 Pet.	1 Peter
Rev.	Revelation		

CONTENTS

Chapter 1: How Busy Are You? 1
Chapter 2: The Creation 11
Chapter 3: When Right Is Wrong 19
Chapter 4: What Do We Need? 33
Chapter 5: Important Reading 43
Chapter 6: People Look at Things Differently 59
Chapter 7: Sexual Immorality 65
Chapter 8: The Seventy Weeks of Daniel 81
Chapter 9: Church Age 99
Chapter 10: Tribulation, End-Time Tribulation, Great
              Tribulation 111
Chapter 11: The Rapture 123
Chapter 12: John to Share 139
Chapter 13: Overview of Revelation 141
Chapter 14: The Generation When Israel Becomes a Nation 195
Chapter 15: Do You Know? 201

CHAPTER 1

How Busy Are You?

THE CHURCH YOU SERVE IN, what size is it? Large churches have their place and can be very effective in reaching the lost for Christ. You can know the character of the assembly as you can see the heart of the people. Look at the basics.

First, what percentage of people attending the assembly are doing what needs to be done? There are 80 percent working and 20 percent spectating. Almost all churches fall into this range. The only problem is they get the numbers wrong. There are 20 percent working and 80 percent spectating. There should be 100 percent doing the work and 0 percent spectating. God provides jobs for everyone. It doesn't matter if you're a man, woman, child, whether young or old, anywhere in between; there are no exceptions! God has a job for each one of us.

You need to know the goals and objectives of your fellowship. If you don't, then ask and seek God's will. Search out what He wants you to accomplish. Not the other person, you. He put you where you are for a reason. If you don't know what you should be doing, find out and start doing it. The Lord will lead you. When the church and all of us are onboard, going in the same direction, things always work out better. When you let God be the one in charge, in control of the fellowship, your life, everything, will work together for the good.

IS THERE TIME

> And we know that all things work together for the good to those who love God, to those who are called according to His purpose. (Rom. 8:28 NKJV)

The Lord has a plan for each of us, so search for it. Find out what it is for you. Do so, and you will bless the ones you come in contact with, as God has blessed you. We all should work toward His design, not ours and just try to integrate God into it. The kingdom of God must be forward-looking. God has something for each of us to do. If you are not doing anything in your local church, in missions, or reaching out to others, you need to reach out and touch a person for God. Ministry is touching someone's life, and they see Christ. This is important (think about it and remember it). Regardless of what we do, Christ gets the glory, not us. If we get the glory, something is wrong, because the glory belongs to Christ.

How does a person learn what to do? You inquire, pray, and listen. It's very essential for you to hear the Lord, and He will answer you. I can't overemphasize how important listening is. You begin by speaking to Go. Let Him speak to you. Wait for Him to tell you what He wants you to do. He will let you know what you should be doing. Only ask if you're serious. Then hold on for the time of your life. He will show you; and you can trust God because God is greater than all of us, any problem, and any obstacle.

First, nowhere in the Bible does it say that after working so many years, we can stop serving the Lord. You think I don't have to do this anymore? I'm retired and don't have to work anymore. I worked hard all my life, and now it's my turn to rest and do my thing. God never told us to retire from ministering to the needy, sharing with a person who doesn't know God, and praying for others. It does not matter your age, health, or wealth; you can serve in one of the three listed above. It says we are to be about our Father's business until He returns for His church or we go to be with Him. If you are reading this, your time of service is still required by our Lord. This mandate is from God, not man.

Second, where does the cash go? I know, taboo subject. Are the finances being used in our ministries and supporting missions at home and abroad? Or are we spending it on promoting staff and big beautiful structures? Is the debt on the buildings and the wages on employees outweigh the money spent on reaching the lost? We need to ask the question. Are we attempting to reach the lost, or do we want to be entertained, that keeps up with the world's view of a successful church? The buildings are functional tools to reach the lost. Remember, God looks at the heart—why we do, what we do—not the splendor of what we do.

Third, does the pastor have time for the flock? Is he busy in meetings, doing things that add numbers to his membership? They can reach so many more in sizable groups. Perhaps we should ask ourselves, do we come to know the Lord in a group setting or one-on-one? I understand the concept of a large church and a little church inside the structure of church. In large church, there is worship and praise and Bible teaching. In small church, we pray, study God's word, fellowship with one another. One man cannot do everything—study the Bible, the teachings, the sharing, and the praying for everyone. It is a fine line of where you share one-on-one and minister firsthand with the congregation.

As many people as there are in the congregation, that is how many jobs there are for the pastor and his staff. The larger the church, the harder the one-on-one becomes. It is a fine line between equipping the flock to do the ministry, and being involved in the ministry.

> If you are too busy to spend time with God,
> Then you are busier than He intended you to be.

This statement does not mean doing things, no matter how important the things are, church related or not. It means spending time with God one-on-one, *period*. There is that one-on-one principle again.

When we are doing God's work developing the congregation and doing all the things that it takes to make the assembly function, remember that the church is not the building; it's the people. Have we prepared for the journey? We must decide to clothe ourselves in the full armor of God and practice the fruit of the Spirit every day. Don't rationalize your protection away with a busy agenda.

The truth should wrap around us. The truth is what ties all the weapons together, and God has given these weapons to each of us to use. We are to be sincere about our walk, our speech, and our actions. Don't fall into the trap that the world sets for us by being deceitful, full of hypocrisy, and falseness. The righteousness of Christ, He gave to each Christian, and this blocks whatever the devil throws at us. Satan goes after each Christian in their weakest state, and he knows our weakness. Our resolve must be to put on the armor of God. The armor will protect us as we move forward and proclaim the gospel of peace, which is Christ. Our obedience to God during trials will be putting Him first and putting His word in our lives and accepting His will of love over our will. Faith is relying on the unseen, and the grace of Christ that grants us the shield of our defense. Our salvation is the helmet, which protects us, and our hope is in Him. Faith and applying the word of God is what stops Satan and his attacks on us. When Christians put on their armor, we prepare for the battle ahead, and you can be sure Satan will attack. God provides us with more than defensive weapons. He gives us offensive weapons as well. The sword of the Spirit, which is the word of God, and we find His word in the Bible. We are to always pray. The Bible says, "Pray without ceasing." This means to have an attitude of prayer. Talk to God about everything—the good, the bad, and everything in between. We are to be humble in our prayers. A test to see if your prayers are humble, check to see if they are about you and your wants or are they about yours needs and other's needs. We need to pray in the Spirit. In our own power, we will run out of energy, but in God's power, there is unlimited energy.

> The Fruit of the Spirit: But the fruit of the Spirit is love, joy, peace, longsuffering, kindness, goodness, faithfulness, gentleness, self-control. Against such there is no law. (Gal. 5:22–23 NKJV)

We are to keep truth at the forefront of our mind and wear righteousness. Christians are to share the gospel of peace. Above all, hold strong to our faith, which will protect us from what the wicked one throws at us. Our salvation is our strength, and the sword of the Spirit is the word of God. Always pray in supplication in the Spirit. Be watchful until the end, with all perseverance for all saints. I will speak and make the gospel known to all. Reference to Ephesians 6:14–19.

Righteousness: the quality of being morally right

Supplication: the action of asking for something earnestly or humbly

May I open my mouth and boldly make known the mystery of the gospel.

The Fruits of the Spirit

love	joy	peace
long-suffering	kindness	goodness
faithfulness	gentleness	self-control

The Armor of God

Girded your waist with truth
Put on the breastplate of righteousness
Shod your feet with the preparation of the gospel of peace
The shield of faith
The helmet of salvation
The sword of the Spirit
Praying always

Many people think the journey is in doing all the tasks of the assembly and persuade others to believe. Our job is to share Christ with all the people we encounter. Our job is not to make someone accept Christ; it is to relate our experience of Christ to others. The Holy Spirit's job is to convict him, or her, of their sins. We are to be an example, a witness for Christ. Everyone has a story. We must share Christ with those we come into contact with in our words and actions. They go together.

Our role in the church is to be mentoring somebody to teach someone how to carry on the ministry. So when God calls us, two things happen. One, we are able and willing to go. Two, the ministry continues without us there. When God wants us to accomplish something, we are to step out in faith and do whatever He asks. Then His kingdom works, and our faith grows. He desires the job He gave us to be completed. Sometimes God moves us out of the path to show everyone who is responsible for the greatness that is happening. The glory always goes to God. It should never be ours. If the credit falls anywhere else than with God, there is a problem, and that problem more than likely is the sin of pride.

God is preparing us in good times and in the trials that we go through. They are all teachable moments. No matter how intelligent we think we are, we can always learn from God's word. There was a man that could recall many facts and stories with great accuracy about the Bible. They were what he learned ten, twenty years ago, but nothing current. So did he quit seeking, or did the Lord stop showing? Our pride in our knowledge from the past limits what the Lord will do in our lives today. The Lord will show us something new every day, if we let Him. As we grow in the Lord, He prepares us for our next assignment. And yes, the Lord has assignments for each of us to do.

How long do people in large churches stay in their position? Have they prepared an individual to carry on with the task in their absence when the Lord gives them their next assignment? When the Lord give us responsibilities, he grants us leadership, but He is the one in charge. We should always follow His leading and mentor someone. When you are mentoring a person, you need to teach, nurture, love, and pray each day for that person! When a ministry is growing and functioning, then the person in charge moves on and the ministry stops. One or more things happened. There could be several things, but here are a couple: the leader in charge didn't mentor someone or the ministry is more about the person in charge rather than about God. In either case, the leader didn't follow or understand God's instructions and directions, or the ministry was more an idea of man's than God's.

Is it possible for someone to stay in a position in the church for too long? Many things reward a person to stay too long, whether in service of the Lord or in the private sector. The money may be too good to look somewhere else, or we just don't hear that still, quiet voice anymore. Maybe the problem is, we become too comfortable. They are not willing to move out of their comfort zone when the Lord says, "Come, I need you here." More often than not, it's the money, not the lack of it but the excess of it. Which can make it almost impossible to hear when Jesus is calling. Money and being humble are two factors that have a hard time going together. Not insurmountable, just hard. The reason this is hard: the more money we make, the more money we want, and the harder it is to be content and hear God speak to us. Money can blind us and affect our hearing. It is hard to stay focused on the Lord's work of sharing Christ when keeping up with your neighbor. All the things related to money can be overwhelming, especially when keeping up with your neighbor. Our eyes are on the world and what it offers in the now instead of on God!

> A servant can only serve one master, no one can serve two. He will hate the one and love the other. He will be loyal to one and despise the other. We cannot serve God and mammon. (Luke 16:13 NKJV)

Mammon: wealth regarded as an evil influence, a false object of worship and devotion, the devil of covetousness.

The key comes with the attitude in which everyone carries out their ministry. God does not look at the task; he looks at our heart: the reason why we do what we do. Our work for the Lord is essential, and faith without works is dead, but the work can never take the place of our relationship with Christ. The work that we do is in His strength, not ours.

Water is the source of all life on this planet, and everything living requires water, and it must keep moving to stay fresh and effective. The best water that I have ever found was in a stream that was moving from place to place. But to be successful in its goal, it must continue to move forward. Water stops only for a while on its journey and affects different places along its path. When water stays in one place for too long, it dies and sours. People are like water. If they stay too long in one place, it becomes stagnant. On the surface, it looks like we are accomplishing what we are supposed to. However, underneath, it is stagnant and dying. The trouble is, we stop listening to that still, quiet voice and begin rationalizing the issue; and then stagnation affects so many things that we touch. All too often, stagnation occurs, and we don't see it coming. From a distance, it looks as if we are doing what He intended us to do. On close inspection, you discover we are not the person who God wanted us to be. God's desire is for us to be successful. To be successful, it has to be His will, not ours. Never substitute our will over His will to make things work out. We need to follow His directions, not ours. So how do you find out what is too long? The key is learning to *listen* to God. The more we communicate with God, the more we will know where we should be. When we change God's plans for our plans, that is where stagnation occurs.

Many individuals are very intelligent, good at organizing plans, and preparing to get things done. More often than not, when people are praying about doing a project for God, we miss a step. We seek guidance. Then we set up a plan to carry out the task. Next, we set things in motions to get the ball rolling. We get people onboard, and pick up the supplies, then launch to accomplish the task. Sounds good, so what step did we miss? After we pray and ask for guidance comes the most important step. I can't emphasize enough how vital this step is. A lot of us miss this step. We have to *wait* and *listen* on the Lord's instructions. If we want this task to be a success and bring glory to God, we have to include the Lord in the planning stage. Almost all of us ask the Lord for guidance, but few of us wait for the Lord's input, unfortunately.

HOW BUSY ARE YOU?

People give all kinds of reasons churches fail. One of the reasons is that people feel comfortable, safe where they are wanted to avoid stepping out of a sure thing into an unknown. They worry about the unknown. And they want to remain in their comfort zone; after all, they are good at what they do. The ones in charge felt very secure where they were and felt that's where they're going to be forever. They didn't prepare anyone to take their place; they didn't mentor anyone. The people no longer listened or heard that still, quiet voice anymore, and they stayed too long. When a person stays too long, you are too busy being busy, and you cannot hear God's voice say, "I need you to go here." God put us in a place for a time to learn, to grow, to teach, to share, and to touch someone's life. Then God will say, "Come," then you step out in faith, and He moves you and takes care of you. If we have followed His instructions, the ministry will continue and thrive after we have moved on. Remember, God is in charge, not us.

It's not about people remembering us; it's about people remembering God, Jesus, and what He has done. We know we have done what God wanted us to do when we leave a ministry and it continues and grows. It is not when we accomplish all the things we have set out on our list, but when we prepare someone to do the job as we proceed to the next thing God has for us to do. While we are doing our ministry, God is preparing us for what is next. So mentor someone before that still, small voice says, "It's your time to move." Now this is important: God gets the glory, not us! Let me repeat that: God gets the glory! This simple fact has to be at the very core of what we are doing in ministry.

There is a fine line between encouraging people and giving them the glory. God is the one who acts through us. He may call you to spend your life doing a certain ministry. God may call you to start a ministry and get it underway and someone else finishes it. He requires us to mentor someone, teach and share what God has shown us. God wants us to grow, and we grow by stepping out in faith. The key factor is, we *listen to God*. Make sure that when we get in the middle of accomplishing these significant tasks for God that we do not become the leader, that God remains the leader. Remember, God looks at the heart. God wants to have fellowship with us, with you, so fellowship with him along the way. Communicate with Him. He looks forward to hearing from you and me, and He will listen to us and respond to us. Sounds like maybe it would be okay to pray more than once a day.

CHAPTER 2

The Creation

GOD FORMED THE OCEANS, LAKES, rivers, mountains, valleys, plants, fish, birds, and animals on earth. He designed all things outside of the earth: sun, moon, stars, and the space that we see and that we can't see. He created all that lives, breaths, and grows. If it creeps, walks, flies, swims, He created it—and everything in this world. He made man, and that was the crown of God's creation. Man is in the image of God.

> Then God said, "Let us make man in Our image, according to Our likeness, let them have dominion over the fish of the sea, over the birds of the air, and over the cattle, over all the earth and over every creeping thing that creeps on the earth." (Gen. 1:26 NKJV)

Our relationship to God differs from any of His other creations. We are not like the angels in heaven; the animals on earth; the birds of the air; and the fish of the oceans, rivers, and streams. God made humans in His image. In His image, that makes us special in relation to everything else He created. When God said, "Let us make man in Our image," let us and our image tells us that someone was there in the beginning with God. Christ and the Holy Spirt was there with God in the beginning. The Trinity has always been God the Father, God the Son, and God the Holy Spirit—three in one.

Man is the dominant creature on this planet. And God gave man authority over all living things. Man had great responsibly from God. God worked for six days in creating everything. However, the seventh day was different. He showed us something essential about work. He rested from it. We are to follow His example. It shows us what we should do in our lives, and that is to rest one of the seven days. By resting, when we come back to work, we will be stronger. It is a time to reset our mind and body to reignite a strength in all of us. So we can go about accomplishing what God has set out for us to do. Yes, God has something for each of us to do. When we take time to refresh our mind and body, it gives us time to reflect on our actions, thoughts, and desires. That's what make us who we are. To refocus on getting self out of the way and to be able to see more clearly that Christ is the one that needs to be in charge. Things will always go better when we let Christ be the one in charge of our life.

Each one of us has a purpose in this life. It doesn't matter if you are a preacher, deacon, teacher, group leader, greeter, custodian, or part of the congregation, God has something for all of us to do. I believe the Lord has two purposes for each of us. *First*, we are to fellowship with the Father. God desires to have fellowship with His children. He will not force us to fellowship with Him. He has always wanted and still wants to have fellowship with man. The Lord created us for fellowship. It is man's choice if he wishes to fellowship with God. *Second*, we all have something to do. He made us all with very special abilities. God put you where you are for a specific reason. We are in this place to be used by God. Yes, we are to be used! All of us owe everything to God. So serve the Lord with joy as the Holy Spirit leads you.

Adam and Eve listened to Satan rather than being obedient to God. They sinned. The first sin of this world came from Adam and Eve. That sin broke the fellowship they had with God. Sin caused, and will always cause, separation between man and God. God will not tolerate or rationalize sin to be okay. The definition of sin is disobedience to God. We are God's creation, and He is to do with us as He sees fit. He could have eliminated us and started all over, but His love for us was so great that He did the unthinkable: He made a way. Out of God's love for each of us, He provided a way to enter into a right relationship with Him. The way back to God is Jesus Christ, the only way to God.

> Jesus said to him, "I am the way, the truth, and the life. No one comes to the Father except through Me." (John 14:6 NKJV)

Since God created everything, He is the only reason we have all the things that we find so dear to our heart, our worldly possessions. Having money and a lot of great, expensive possession is not sin, but the importance we attach to them can make them sin. Possessions have nothing to do with success. Non-Christians think in terms of worldly possessions to gauge how successful they have become. Unfortunately, there are Christians who think the same way. They don't realize that this attitude is a sin attitude, not a Christ attitude. Having things is not a sin in its self. Possessions are not how God judges success.

Christ looks at a person's heart, and character is the gauge that shows how successful a person has become. It's never about the money; it's always about the heart. Character is how we react to the situations that happen to us in this life and the decisions that we make. Between personal possessions and character, character is more important to God every time. Our character is one of those unique things that connects us to God and makes us who He wants us to be. We don't develop character by ourselves; it is given by the Holy Spirit. We must embrace character in order that it may become a reality in our lives.

God instructed man that he has to take care of the garden. One of the things God told man was not to eat from the tree of knowledge of good and evil. That sin nature that we see today started back with Adam and Eve's disobedience. They had a choice, and they chose wrong. You see the effect of their choice on our children as you watch them grow. You tell them, "Now don't do this," and they do what you told them not to do. We see the sin nature coming through that everyone was born with. Satan deceived man and woman, and to this day, we have learned little about evil and the lies that he spreads to all of us. When they eat from the tree of knowledge of good and evil, they were being disobedient to God. The proper name for disobedience to God is sin. Humans over and over have disobeyed God. We seem to be very slow learners. People give every rational reason, every excuse, every act of tolerance. Give it whatever name you want, disobedience to God is sin, *period*!

We carry sin down from generation to generation by man's seed. Man is the one who is responsible for what happens in the family. Man has disobeyed God time and time again. But God's love for each of us is demonstrated in His willingness to accept us back into His loving grace. I love the acronym of grace: *God's Riches At Christ Expense* or *God's Resources And Christ Experiences*. God's love has no limits, no limitation whatsoever. Amen!

One day, when Christ returns, He will bring justice to this world; and the influence of Satan will end. Satan will have no more power over us. This will be a time of rejoicing when sin is no longer in the world, only God's love. Now that's a day to look forward to.

Christ gives all of us joy when we accept Him as Lord and Savior. I think most people misunderstand joy. Joy and happiness are related, but they are not the same thing. Joy is from a relationships and happiness is from our circumstances. In our relationship to the Lord, He gives us joy, not man. Our circumstances cannot take joy from us. If things are going well—finances, job, and friends around us, with little or no problems—we are happy. The joy of the Lord cannot be taken from us, but we can lose our happiness through our circumstances. Joy stays with us, but happiness comes and goes.

To understand joy that Christians have, we need to look at how joy works in your life. We must put *J*esus first, *O*thers second, *Y*ourself third, which brings joy to our life: *Jesus—Others—Yourself.*

Christians are to endure through the trials and problems of this world. God does not remove us from the trials and tribulations that come our way. This is where Christians build character. Character comes from the Holy Spirit. Christians are to remain faithful to the end to our creator, God. Believers are to stand fast in our faith, in the strength of our Lord Jesus Christ. Our worship is due Him and no other, only God. Followers of Christ are not to worship other gods or put other gods above Him. People will be able to tell where your allegiance is by the love that radiates from within you. Christians are to keep their heart and attitude focused on God and on the things of God. Coming to know the Lord is a personal experience, not a group event. It can happen in a group, but the conversion is one-on-one, you and the Lord. It isn't and has never been our responsibility to convince people of their sins—that job is for the Holy Spirit. Our job is to tell people about Jesus, the ones the Lord puts in our path. We are to tell them what He has done in our life, not someone else's life, our life. We are to follow Christ's example. He loves the person, not the sin; *we are to love the person, not the sin*. Not only that, we need to know our Lord personally and seek His will in our life. Have you ever wondered how you can know what the will of God is in your life? God has so much in store for us, and he reveals His will to each of us, through His word (the Bible).

There are several places in the Bible that talk about the will of God for our lives. Here are three basic principles of being in God's will.

> Rejoice evermore. Pray without ceasing. In everything give thanks: for this is the will of God in Christ Jesus concerning you. (1 Thess. 5:16–18 NKJV)

Rejoice evermore: we are to rejoice always. We are to have an attitude of joy. When we are in His will, we will have joy.

Pray without ceasing: this does not mean all we do is pray, it means we have a prayerful attitude. Prayer is nothing more than talking to God. We need to seek God in a prayerful and humble attitude.

Give thanks in everything: we are to be thankful in all things. God is controlling all things, and we are to have a thankful attitude about what the Lord is doing in our life.

Each one of these three are actions that we are to be doing. These attitudes are to be developed by each one of us. You didn't know that having an attitude was a good thing. God wants us to be happy. He looks at our heart, not our actions. He wants us to rejoice, pray, and be thankful. All of us are to trust in the Lord that He has put us right where He wants us. God has put us in this place, at this time, for a reason.

When Adam and Eve disobeyed God, they introduced sin into the world. Now we are born with a sinful nature, which separates us from God. Christ is the only way to overcome sin. He is the only bridge that can span the gulf that was created between man and God. Jesus paid the price for our sins so we could have fellowship with our Lord. Christ is the Messiah that the Jews were waiting for. Christ died on the cross for our sins, Christ was born of a virgin, Christ rose form the dead, and Christ lives today with the Father in heaven. He will return one day for the chosen and the faithful.

> These will make war with the Lamb, and Lamb will overcome them, for He is Lord of lords and King of kings; and those who are with Him are called, chosen, and faithful. (Rev. 17:14 NKJV)

Who are the chosen and the faithful? The chosen are the Jews, and the faithful is His church. These two groups are the ones who are believers in Jesus Christ. Just because you are a Jew or citizen of a country or a member of a local church, it does not grant you entrance into heaven. No one will enter the kingdom of God except through Jesus Christ.

Christ differs from every other man who has, is, or ever will be on this planet. He entered the same way as you and I entered this world, from the womb of woman. The difference is, Christ was born of a virgin. He is not from the seed of man. Jesus is not of a sin nature. Christ has always been the Son of God and has been with

THE CREATION

God from the beginning. When Christ walked on earth as man, He had all the growing pains as you and I had as a child. He was hungry, needing to eat, and thirsty, needing to drink. He went through all the things boys go through as a child. Joseph and Mary knew of the greatness that was in their midst and of the great task and honor that God had given them. God gave Joseph and Mary a great blessing, the care of His Son, Jesus Christ.

Does Satan attack Christians who don't engage and remain on the sidelines? Does Satan go after those who seek to serve Christ? Satan attacks anyone who is serving Christ and making a difference. Christians will offend people because of the message of Jesus Christ that we share with them. Christians never want to offend people but are not to worry about offending people to the point that they do not share Christ with others. It is not the other guy's responsibility. We are to share. There are confused and dying people out there without Christ in their life. Everyone will spend eternity in one of two places, and that's heaven or hell. Satan has masked this lifestyle of sin as being great and desirable. Don't be deceived, that life also comes with great pain.

If you are a Christian, what persecution are you enduring for Jesus Christ? If not, then how effective is your witness for Christ? The world will persecute whoever tells them about the truth, and the truth is Jesus Christ. When they see the Father's love in us and see us trying to serve Him, the persecution will come. Persecution is to discourage you and try to stop you from sharing Christ. Christ was persecuted because He came to save people from their sins. The persecution that Christians endure is for living a life that follows our Lord Jesus Christ.

Jesus is speaking: "The world hated Me before it hated you. If you were of the world, it would love its own." Christ said, "I chose you out of the world, and it hates you because of that. Remember, a servant is not greater than His master. They persecuted Me, so they will persecute you. They will do all these things to you because of My name's sake. They don't know My Father. If I had not come they would not have sin but they have no excuse for their sin now. They hate Me, so they hate My Father. When I did the works among you that no one else did and they hate you, they have sinned. This was to fulfill what was written in the law. They hated Me without a cause." Reference to John 15:18–25.

Jesus came to serve, not to be served. Christ came to fulfill the Father's will by showing great love and providing a way back to the Father for all men. Christ's sacrifice on the cross demonstrated His love for all of us and His obedience to the Father. When Christ walked upon the earth as man, He was sinless and obedient of His service to His Father. Everything that Christ did was with no sin. Service is the action that shows the true nature of the heart. God looks at our heart, at our attitude, and the reason we do what we do. God knows the difference from true service of the heart to going through the motions to impress.

But Jesus called them to Himself and said, "You know that the rulers of the Gentiles lord it over them, and those who are great exercise authority over them. Yet it shall not be so among you; but whoever desires to become great among you, let him be your servant. And whoever desires to be first among you, let him be your slave-just as the Son of Man did not come to be served, but to serve, and to give His life a ransom for many." Reference to Matthew 20:25–28.

CHAPTER 3

When Right Is Wrong

WE ARE ALWAYS TRYING TO size up new people that we meet. The first impression we get from each of us is never right, because of the way people put up false impressions of who they are. We all want to impress those with whom we come into contact with. When we begin to show our true self, with our guard down, people get a glimpse of who we are. This is like when people marry. You and your spouse look at each other for the first time, the real you, not the one you show to impress. In your mind, you go, *Oh!* Example: The first morning the happy couple get up and start getting ready for the day, and all of a sudden, one of you sees the other person a little differently, and little things start to happen. Could be their appearance, what they look like before they get ready, or some little thing that as you are around them just annoys you, or one person drinks the milk from the bowl after the cereal and the other doesn't. Some of the littlest things that don't matter begin to make a difference in the way we look at each other. That's why there is a time of getting used to each other in almost every marriage. Generally, but not always, your spouse sees this person and thinks, Where did the person I was dating go? Where did this strange person come from that looks just like the person I dated and then married? During the first few months, or a year, our love and commitment to each other take over and the little things just don't matter anymore. Your love for each other grows stronger with each passing day. Then one day you realize you have been married for twenty, thirty, forty years and you can't think of living one day without the love of your life, the one you married so many years ago.

Even with friends, we try hard to impress and not show who we are. When we let our true self out, you become worried, because you are exposing who you are for another human to see. That can be an eye-opening experience when you realize it. When people get a good look at the real you, they get a unique glimpse into our lives. Most people are afraid to show who they are. People don't deal with rejection well. That short, revealing glimpse will tell people if they want to know more about you or want to disappear as fast as they can. For some people, it is a stroll down memory lane. For others, it is a walk down a path of "I've been there, done that, and no way that is ever happening again." They are so afraid of being hurt that they miss touching someone's life and someone touching their life in such a strong, positive way. If we don't deal with the fear, we will miss the friend that God sends our way.

Everyone puts up a front. That way your true self doesn't get put out there for all to see. When we put up this front, it's just for appearance, and it shows everything is just fine. It's like a built-in self-protection of our self-esteem to hide the true person, never letting anyone see who we are. If you think back a few thousand years ago, man crucified the only perfect one that ever walked on this planet. We are just self-conscious and don't want anyone to know or even appear that we have any issues. All of us have this built-in self-protection mechanism that tries to keep us from getting hurt, rejected, or both.

Have you ever been around someone, and they impress you? The first time you meet this person, you think, Now that person has it all together. I wish I had my life together like that. You ask yourself the question, Why can't I be like that? But after a short time of being around them, a brief time, you see they didn't quite have it all together as you thought.

WHEN RIGHT IS WRONG

Too often we give a total stranger this perfect image of who we are. You project to others who you think they prefer to see. We never reveal our imperfections, always showing our best, letting no one see the real you. There is always that fear that they won't like what they see and reject us. One of the greatest fears man has is rejection. No one wants to be rejected by somebody; everybody desires to be accepted. We all want friends, someone we can trust to share things of personal interest and concerns with, someone you can confide in. When we meet people for the first time, I think we all put each person into different categories. When we are younger, there is no such thing as a stranger. But when we are older, we worry about what that person thinks of us, or will they take advantage of us, or will they hurt us in some way? It's just a new friend when you're younger. When we grow older, we start to categorize people a little more. Maybe we are taught this as a self-protection mode in our lives. Most people don't intend to categorize the people they encounter; it just happens.

When people do these things, they miss finding a good friend, the one that God sent their way. To find a true friend—now that has its risks. The catch is, you must become one. This means you have to show your true self. So take a chance and be a friend. Show someone the real you. You might be surprised at their response. Yes, there will always be those jerks that make themselves feel better at the expense of others. But sometimes you find that person who has the potential to be that loyal friend. This person is worth the risk. Most people are seeking a friend, somebody they can share all their little secrets with. So find someone in need, and be that friend.

> A friend loves at all times, and a brother is born for adversity. (Prov. 17:17 NKJV)

A True Friend

> A true friend, true friendship, is a great treasure to hold on to and never, never, abuse that friendship and always be true to the friend.

> A true friend will always be truthful with you, even when it hurts.
> A true friend will always seek to build you up.
> A true friend will always find the best in what you do.
> A true friend will always be there for you, to share in the good times, and to help in the bad times.
> A true friend is worth more than all the money, gold, and silver in this world.
> A true friend will bring you joy.

If you find a true friend, then God has smiled on you.
If you find two, you are blessed.

There's only been one perfect man in this world. I know there are one or two of you who think they're perfect, but there's only been one. We all have imperfections and flaws. Oh, that perfect man, we crucified Him. Yes, you and I, the person sitting next to you, the person you have not met yet, the person who was there—we all crucified Him, Jesus Christ. If you have ever sinned, your sin connects you to the crucified Christ, and the Bible says all have sinned. You and I had a part in the crucifying of Jesus Christ. It's everybody's sin, which Christ died for on the cross. Have you ever thought about what it would be like to meet a person who was what they appeared to be? The first meeting you had with them, you get the same impression as the last. There was one many years ago that was like that. What you saw was what you got, the real thing.

Jesus Christ

Jesus wants us to be happy and successful in everything we do for Him. What is the strategy for successful living? The world would have us believe that a generous bank account and the money to buy whatever you want is the mark of a successful person. Perhaps it is having a large beautiful home and the stylish furnishings, or the car of your dreams, or awesome truck that puts your neighbors to shame, or maybe it's that RV and being able to travel whenever you feel like it. When we look closely at the people who have accomplished most of these things, you will find that they don't seem happy. If they do seem happy, it is usually superficial. They seem more occupied with keeping those things and acquiring more. Their focus seems to be more on things rather than Jesus. Things don't bring us joy, and the more things we acquire, the more things control us. It's like an addiction: to get more and better than our neighbor. The more things we acquire, the harder it is to be content with what we have and with our life. There is nothing wrong with having things. But it's the attention, attitude, the desire that we place on these things that can make them sin. But where do you balance between your possessions and Jesus. Example: if you are a huge football fan and your team made it to the Super Bowl and they changed the time to eleven on Sunday morning, where would you be, in church or in front of that big-screen TV? When we learn to be content with what we have, we begin to take the first step toward success. Being content and having character is true success.

We all seem to be so self-involved in knowledge and being able to explain everything that we miss one of the greatest mysteries of our existence. The mystery of all time is that a higher being is in control, and we don't always have to be the one with all the answers. Perhaps it is best if someone besides you and me have the answers, one who is all powerful and all-knowing—God!

> In God's strategy for successful living
> Character is more important than intelligence.

Character is something everyone can have, regardless of their intelligence, wealth, or health. God gives character and is developed by the Holy Spirit within us. What is Christian character and what does it look like? In the book of Galatians, it talks about walking in the Spirit. The Holy Spirit dwells within us when we become followers of Christ. He comes to comfort and guide every Christian.

IS THERE TIME

Each of us is justified by our faith and has peace with God in our Lord Jesus Christ. We have access by faith in His grace and rejoice in hope in God's glory. We also glory in tribulation, and tribulation produces perseverance, and perseverance produces character, and character produces hope. Reference to Romans 5:1–5.

> But the fruit of the Spirit is love, joy, peace, longsuffering, kindness, goodness, faithfulness, gentleness, self-control. Against such there is no law. (Gal. 5:22–23 NKJV)

> Self-effort doesn't produce Christian character; the Holy Spirit produces and develops character within us.

When will the truth be wrong, and the lie be right? There will be a time when the majority accepts the lie and not the truth. God's word is truth. His word is the same yesterday, today, and forever. The world and its values change, but God's truth and justice and love never do. God's love goes out to everyone, and He is just and true to His word. When things change, God is not the one who changed.

We need to confess our sins and ask forgiveness for them. Don't rationalize sin into an acceptable way of life. Just because our society thinks they are more open, tolerant, and enlightened, they think sin is okay. No matter how smart men get and what excuses they give for their sins that they commit, sin is sin to God. The world says that some sinful actions are okay. Remember, sin is disobedience to God. You either obey God or you disobey God. It's that simple. *Sin is never okay to God.* Sin is never a right of ours. It's a conscious decision on our part to disobey God. When men stop hiding their sin and displaying it for all to see and claiming it is there right to do what the Bible says is sin. God will judge one day and will not rationalize sin to be acceptable.

The world is more concerned about our individual rights rather than right or wrong. God is more concerned with right or wrong than with our individual rights. He is the creator and master of the universe. What we possess is only because God gave it to us. We are His creation and His to do with as He pleases. The Bibles view of sin is its disobedience to God, but the world views it as a person's choice. The world believes everyone needs to be more open and tolerant. Remember God's view, and it doesn't matter how the world rationalizes it. *Sin is sin, no exceptions, none!*

When people decide to disobey God, His judgment will come one day. His love is available to all that will listen to His word. "He who has an ear, let him hear what the Spirit says to the churches"—this is repeated several times in chapter 2 and 3 of the book of Revelations. There will come a time when most people are convinced by a few that sin is right. The time will come when being a Christian, and standing up for Christ will not be acceptable. Will Christians stand for what's right? God's word is right! Men will deny what is in the Bible. Some people who claim to be a Christians do so because it's the accepted thing to do now, but that will change one day.

How long before our country joins the one-world socialism or one-world government? Socialism (communism) is the government ruling the people, not the people controlling the government. How long do you think it will be before the powers to be want to track and arrest hate crime individuals? Christians don't have to be concerned with hate crimes. They focus on love and helping others, right? Could the Bible, our actions and beliefs, look like hate crimes? The world can rationalize any view to look good or hateful. What will happen to Christians who speak what the Bible reveals about sin? Speaking what the Bible says will be a hate crime one day. Will Christian stand for God, or will they be silent because they fear retaliation? Make no mistake, Satan will test our faith more and more the closer we get to end times. Is your faith in God a relationship or fire insurance?

Our individual rights are essential; that's what makes this country great. We have always held the right to believe in God. The government is to say out of the church but not the influence of the church on the government. In the world's view, there are no difference between churches and cults. In God's view, it is as different as Christ and Satan.

Church—it is a group of people that believe that Christ is the Messiah. The followers of Christ, the bride of Christ, they believe that He is the Savior of humanity. In God's grace, Christ is the Savior of the world. Jesus Christ is God's Son. Christians serve a risen Savior. Christ is the Messiah and sent the Holy Spirit to be with us until He returns for His church. The only way to be a part of the church is to accept Christ as your personal Lord and Savior. Nobody goes to the Father except through Christ.

Cults—cults have followers and believers of Satan, not God. A cult resembles a church in appearance only and how it operates. The difference is, they don't believe in Christ's authority or that he is the Messiah. Most cults believe that Christ was a good teacher. They deny Christ as God's Son. Individual rights are more important than right or wrong. Their members believe that they can be as gods. Cult members believe Satan is god. They don't fear God; they fear Satan. Cult members believe Satan is the way to heaven. Heaven is not Satan's to give.

Our personal rights can take us out of the realm of right or wrong. This incorrectly leads us toward personal rights and causes pain in our lives. We go down a path of self-indulgence. This sin lets us rationalize an unacceptable behavior and makes sin look right. Sin is no longer sin for us because as an individual, our personal rights are more important than right or wrong. God looks at it as sin is sin, no matter how man rationalize it. God looks at right or wrong as more critical than our personal rights.

God will punish our self-indulgent path one day. There is no way He will let sin run free and unchecked. Sin leads people away from what they know to be true and right. Who would be the mastermind behind this great deception? This deceiver has used many names over the years: Satan, Lucifer, and, in the future, the Antichrist. Everyone is born with a sin nature, but we are also born with the ability to decide if we will sin or not. People claim they can worship God and still rationalize sin as okay. They claim to be worshiping God; they deceive themselves. God cannot and will not be a part of sin. The mastermind behind this great deception is the one they are worshiping, Satan.

WHEN RIGHT IS WRONG

A few years back, the family was a powerful force in the United States. The household had a solid biblical foundation built into the structure, with good morals and beliefs. Family: a man (husband), a woman (wife), children (boy/girl). Even families who were not Christian and attending a local church, they had these essential truths built into their lives. God's principles were there to make the family strong and united. They may not have known what these basic beliefs were, but they were so ingrained in their way of life that they strived to reach them.

There was a struggle between the Soviet Union (Russia) and the United States (America), the two biggest superpowers of the world. Russia said, at one time, there was only one way to defeat America, and it was not by firing a shot. The strongest thing in America is the family. It's what ties it all together. If America was to fall, the family had to be noneffective. They believed that the family is the strong moral fabric of America. It is the glue that gives it its strength. When you destroy the family, America will fall. The way for a nation to stay free is to be the strongest military out there and with a commander with the wisdom to know when and when not to use it. If the military and the leader go weak, so will the country. There will be nothing to stop evil from overtaking that country and then the world. Evil has vowed to kill anyone who does not believe, think, and act as they do. They believe it is their right and obligation to stop and destroy any person or nation that stands against their beliefs. One day the good will become the criminal and the immoral become the upright in the eyes of the general population—the wicked will see to it.

Evil keeps us busy doing things that appear to be of God. When the church doors open and the assembly meets, there is one who never misses: Satan and some of his servants (demons). The times we don't get along and have problems, he is always there to cause chaos every time. Satan is careful to leave the plan of salvation out of the services that he controls. Anything involved in doing things more than telling the lost about Christ, His salvation, is not of God. God gave all of us gifts to use in sharing Jesus Christ with the world. We are to apply our abilities to reach the lost for Christ. The Holy Spirit develops spiritual gifts for each one of us for the profit of all.

IS THERE TIME

All spiritual gifts will benefit believers in the assembly. The Holy Spirit will develop these gifts in different individuals as needed to build up the church. The Bible lists these gifts: the word of wisdom, the word of knowledge, faith, healing, miracles, prophecy, discerning the spirits, tongues, and interpretation of tongues.

The Corinthians exalted the practice of speaking in tongues as especially spiritual, possessed by the Spirit. Some denominations believe that in the day there were groups with several dialects speaking. So when one person would speak, another would interpret what was being spoken to benefit the group.

It does not matter where you fall on this. We all should agree: it is to build up the body and bring unity in diversity.

The word of wisdom	Practical application of knowledge
The word of knowledge	The ability to teach
Faith	To believe God for extraordinary deeds
Healing	Minister to others
The work of miracles	The ability to perform miraculous wonders
Prophecy	The telling of the revelations from God
Discerning	The ability to distinguish the word of God from demonic activity in church
Speaking in tongues	To edify one's self or the congregation. If the congregation, interpretation is required. A dialect that others in the group don't understand.
Interpretation of tongues	The ability to explain or translate the tongues spoken in the congregation

> Therefore I make know to you that no one speaking by the Spirit of God calls Jesus accursed and no one can say that Jesus is Lord except by the Holy Spirit. There are diversities of gifts, but the same Spirit. There are differences of ministries, but the same Lord. And there are diversities of activities, but it is the same God who works

> all in all. But the manifestation of the Spirit is given to each one for the profit of all: for to one is given the word of wisdom through the Spirit, to another the word of knowledge through the same Spirit, to another faith by the same Spirit, to another gifts of healing by the same Spirit, to another the working of miracles, to another prophecy, to another discerning of spirits, to another different kinds of tongues, to another the interpretation of tongues. But one and the same Spirit works all these things, distributing to each one individually as He wills.
>
> For as the body is one and has many members, but all the members of that one body, brings many, are one body, so also is Christ. For by one Spirit we were all baptized into the one body-whether Jews or Greek, whether slaves or free-and have all been made to drink into one Spirit. For in fact the body is not one member but many. (1 Cor. 12:3–14 NKJV)

People can see Christ in our actions, our thoughts, and our words. With Christ, there is something different about us. Christians should not blend in with everyone else. The light of Christ becomes dim when we rationalize sin to be correct. Sin is never correct, and it only destroys. If we live a Christ-centered life, they will want what they see. God never asked us to stay in our comfort zone. Rather, He wants us to step out and show Christ's love in our lives. We are to share our firsthand knowledge and experiences of this wonderful gift that God gave to the world, Jesus Christ. We must speak about what God has done for us.

Satan deceived the ancient world into believing that the Messiah would bring physical peace and His kingdom with Him. Christ came for the first time and brought spiritual peace. The peace that they were seeking will be when He returns for His church. The Jews were looking for a ruler to change the balance of power. They were so obsessed with their self, rules, and regulations that they missed the greatest gift God had ever given them. They missed God's love, the Son God, the Messiah. He paid the ultimate price and walked up the hill and let them nail him to the cross. What a tragedy to be right there by Christ and not see our Lord. And even worse, they crucified Him. My sin is just as bad as their sin because sin is sin to God. We might as well as walked among them, picked up the hammer, and drove the nails in with our own hands. Man puts the degree on sin: this one not so bad, this one is worse. Sin is sin to God.

There is No difference No degrees.

Sin separates us from God!
The only thing that can bridge this separation is Jesus Christ.

Sin will convince people it can take care of all their problems. It will deceive them into thinking that the government will care for them. The government will convince them that they know what is best for them. The government will do what is best for the government, not the people. One-world government, you say that will never happen. What would it required for that to occur? There would have to be a collapse of the financial and the health-care system. Individuals would not put their trust in the systems anymore. The government would intervene, regulate, and control. The next step would be to take control of the airways: television and radio. Then they would need to have control of everything we read: newspapers, magazines, and books. When the government takes over all these mediums, it would set the stage for what is next: control and brainwashing. You think this couldn't take place in our day and age. We are too educated for something like that to occur. They were deceived into believing that the lie is the truth. Everyone has become so much more enlightened to accept the lie as the truth.

> And when you pray, do not use vain repetition
> as heathen do. For they think that they will be
> heard for their many words. (Matt. 6:7 NKJV)

WHEN RIGHT IS WRONG

Evil now has rights, and their rights will overshadow right or wrong. God's word will not be the basis for good or bad, right or wrong. Man's intellect will be. How can sin have rights? Sin is not a right *sin is a conscious decision* and a wrong way of living your life, separated from God. People will believe that a one-world government will take care of them. Humans are a unique kind of being. We choose right or wrong, to worship or not. Man believes what he hears repeatedly. Repetition is the way Satan gets the unwilling to believe the lie. When men hear the lie long enough, men begin to think the lie is the truth.

We established this country many years ago on the right to worship and have fellowship with God. When people think sin has rights, that's a problem. The problem is very basic. It's man's sin, and that's at the core of the problem. A good rule of thumb in solving any problem is to admit there is a problem and return to the basics to resolve the problem. The Bible is the basics, the foundation to building a strong relationship with the greatest problem solver of all time, God! When we leave God out of the equation, that is where sin takes hold and right becomes wrong.

CHAPTER 4

What Do We Need?

THE BIBLE SHOWS THE BEGINNING of time to the end of time. It explains what happened in the past and what is going to happen in the future. How far in the future? No one knows except God. The Bible reveals the purpose of all the books of the Bible. All the books of the Bible point to Jesus Christ as the Savior of the world, the Messiah, and He will return one day for His church. We find the importance as we read all the books in the Bible, and we discover what God's word has to say to us. Something that our culture feels is inappropriate. They say it doesn't apply to us today. I have heard it said that the Bible is for people who cannot make it on their own. They use the Bible as a crutch, and it makes them feel better about themselves and gives them false hope, instead of coming to terms with the world around them. They don't have to deal with reality. The books of the Bible, when read in a prayerful attitude and desire to seek a better life, will enrich and bring joy to the reader every time, without exception.

The Bible affirms where we will be when Christ arrives for the second time. When He returns, it is for every Christian, and He will not leave any behind. Men have been saying the end is coming soon. The end has still not come yet. It must be a long way off, and there is nothing to worry about, right? Wrong! If you don't know Christ as your personal Savior, which means acknowledge and confess your sins, ask Him to forgive your sins, and accept him in your heart to be your Lord, you will not be among those for which he comes back for.

The Bible instructs us about bad and terrible events that occur in the end for humanity. The book also informs us about good things to come, about Christ and the victory He brings with Him upon His return. The Bible, its stories, His parables, its documents, and history—they all point to one thing, Jesus Christ. The Bible reveals Jesus Christ as the Savior of the world, the Messiah.

> The Bible is God's word to man, not man's word about God!

God became man in Jesus Christ. Christ lived among men, had no sin, paid the price for our sins, died on the cross, rose from the dead, and lives today and forever. All men from the time of the cross have access to God *only* through Jesus Christ. Access to God is the same for Jew and Gentile after the cross. Jesus is the *only* way to God.

No matter where you stand in your faith in Christ, your doctrinal beliefs, Paul gave Timothy the key to understanding the Bible: "Study to show thyself approved unto God, a workman that needeth not be ashamed, rightly dividing the word of truth" (2 Tim. 2:15 KJV).

Keys to understanding the Bible: study the Bible, don't be ashamed of the word of God, and know the Bible is God's truth. We are to work on this and do this daily. Let your love and faith stand strong as God's word engulfs you.

There are no set of special rules or secrets for understanding God's word. First, ask that God would reveal His will to you. Then open the Bible and begin reading. If you read with the right attitude and desire in your heart, He will show you what you need. To understand God's will for our lives, we need to have a personal relationship with Jesus Christ. Then the Holy Spirit will guide and mold you into the person God wants you to be. The more you learn about the Father, the Son, and the Holy Spirt, the more you see the Trinity and how they intertwine with each other, three in one.

WHAT DO WE NEED?

The first sixty-five books of the Bible all point to the last one. Each verse, each chapter—all helps reveal the mystery of the last book. The last book's name is Revelation, and that makes sixty-six books in total. The purpose of Revelation is to reveal Jesus Christ as the Savior of humanity, the Messiah.

The Old Testament has thirty-nine books. They are in four major groups: law, history, poetry, and prophets. God has a chosen people. These books show how His chosen people grow with Him and fall away from Him. There are those who show great faith during trials and a time of persecution. They also show how Israel worshiped God. In the Old Testament, the term *salvation* relates to physical deliverance. The major Hebrew verb for *salvation* carries the same meaning of help, deliver, or save. It occurs in eliminating a burden, removing someone from danger, one who hears the cry of the mistreated and liberates them.

The New Testament has twenty-seven books, and they are in four major groups: gospel, history, letters, and apocalypse. This shows Jesus's life—from His birth, His ministry, His death, His resurrection, to His return. It explains Christ and His relationship to the church. It tells the stories of the first churches and reveals the trials and the victory that Christ has over sin in the world.

What is the church? It's believers, followers of Christ, the saints. Never confuse the building as the church. The building is where the church meets. You and I are witnesses to what Christ has done in our life. The Bible will instruct the disciples of Christ. Revelation will tell Christians what will take place very soon: "From that time Jesus began to preach and to say, Repent, for the kingdom of heaven is at hand" (Matt. 4:17 NKJV). Jesus was, and is, at hand. Jesus was, and is, near. The kingdom of heaven refers to the New Testament of God's heavenly kingdom coming to earth in the person of Jesus Christ. It does not mean that Jesus will appear in a few minutes, a few hours, a few days, a few months, or a few years. It means He can come. His arrival is in God's timing. No one knows the day or hour of His return. The only thing we know is we are to be ready.

The New Testament concept of salvation includes most of the elements of the Old Testament and adds spiritual dimensions. There is a personal deliverance from sin. There is spiritual and eternal deliverance through repentance. The New Testament talks of God's power to deliver us from the bondage of sin. There is a future deliverance for believers in Christ when He returns.

The Seven Beatitudes of Revelation

1. "*Blessed* is he who reads and those who hear the words of this prophecy and keep the things which are written in it; for the time is near" (Rev. 1:3 NKJV).

    Blessed are the people reading, listening, and hearing God's word every day. The blessings come from Jesus, engulfing each one us and making Him a part of our lives. We are different in the way we speak, act, and live. We see the good where we were sure there were none before. Christ changes our life for the better. We must be ready for our Lord's arrival. The Lord's return can happen at any time. The time of His return is near.

2. "Then I heard a voice from heaven saying to me, 'Write: "*Blessed* are the dead who die in the Lord from now on." 'Yes,' says the Spirit, 'that they may rest from their labors, and their works follows them'" (Rev. 14:13 NKJV).

    God has the best retirement plan of all, and that's when we leave to be with Him in heaven, then we will rest from our labors. Until that moment, we are to share Christ with others. God put us here for a specific reason. You are the one that can reach that person. When we let God work through us, His blessings flow. On His return, we will be with Him forever. Our labor will be complete at the end of days. We are the clay, and He is the potter. It takes an entire lifetime to shape us to be what He intends us to be. All we have to do is surrender to His will. More of you, Lord, and less of me in control.

WHAT DO WE NEED?

3. "Behold, I am coming as a thief. *Blessed* is he who watches, and keeps his garments, least he walk naked and they see his shame" (Rev. 16:15 NKJV).

    His return is unknown to all. Only one knows the time. And that one is God. We are to be ready, watching for our Lord. We are not to fall into the trap of sin that says, "It's okay, everyone is doing it." And they wear things, and sometimes it is the lack of what they wear, that is not acceptable to God. He does expect us to honor Him with what we say, do, and wear. All should show respect and honor to God. In our walk with Christ, nothing should bring shame into our relationship. It does not matter what people say. Never be ashamed of our Lord. All should bring honor and glory, because He deserves our honor and praise.

4. "Then he said to me, 'Write: "*Blessed* are those who are called to the marriage supper of the Lamb!"' And he said to me, 'These are the true sayings of God'" (Rev. 19:9 NKJV).

    Christ is the groom. We are the bride of Christ, the church (saints). We will be at the marriage supper of our Lord and Savior, Jesus Christ. God's word is true. It is from the one who lives, Jesus Christ. All things will pass away, but His word will never pass away, it will be forever.

5. "*Blessed* and holy is he who has part in the first resurrection. Over such the second death has no power, but they shall be priest of God and of Christ and shall reign with Him a thousand years" (Rev. 20:6 NKJV).

    All Christians will have a part in the first resurrection. We will remain always with Christ. Anyone not found in the book of life, a non-Christian, will be a part of the second resurrection and will live eternally in hell with Satan, separated from God forever. The second resurrection has no power over the ones in the first resurrection. All who are called to the first resurrection will reign with Christ forever.

6. "Behold, I am coming quickly! *Blessed* is he who keeps the words of the prophecy of this book" (Rev. 22:7 NKJV).

    Christ is coming soon. He left us a guide to show us the way until His return. We must keep His words that are in the Bible. He gave us His prophecy to enrich our lives so they may be full and rewarding.

7. "*Blessed* are those who do His commandments, that they may have the right to the tree of life, and may enter through the gates into the city" (Rev. 22:14 NKJV).

    We are to follow His commandments and instructions that he gave us so we would know how to act in this life. The reward is great that the Lord has prepared for us.

> Jesus answered him, "The first of all the commandments is: 'Hear, O Israel, the Lord our God, The Lord is one. And you shall love the Lord your God with all your heart, with all your soul, with all your mind, and with all your strength.' This is the first commandment. And the second, like it, is this: 'You shall love your neighbor as yourself.' There is no other commandment greater than these." (Mark 12:29–31 NKJV)

The first commandment is that we are to love the Lord our God with all our heart, mind, soul, and strength. And the second commandment is, we are to love our neighbor as ourselves. These two are the greatest commandments that the Lord has given each of us. The thing we need to realize is the two greatest commandments are about God and others, not self. The problem we have is, we are a self-centered being. That's why God gave us these commandments and an example of what true love is. Jesus submitted to the Father's will, and that is what we need to do, submit to Him, to stay in His love and grace. We can do all things, from the easy to the impossible, in God's will. We need to let Jesus's light shine through us, to a world in darkness and great need.

WHAT DO WE NEED?

> This is My commandment, that you love one another as I have loved you. Greater love has no one than this, than to lay down one's life for his friends. (John 15:12, 13 NKJV)

This is another commandment of extreme significance. We are to love one another as Christ loved us. Christ laid down His life for every person, and Christ's relationship to us is of great importance to Him and our development. Knowledge alone is not enough. It takes a personal relationship. Then we will show Christ's love as it shines through us. Important: not our love shining out, but Christ's love shining through us!

Adam and Eve were in harmony with God. They were happy without the knowledge of good and evil, with God taking care of them, and with their relationship with God. They were at peace in the garden. Then Satan came to Eve, then Eve to Adam. They made a mistake. They disobeyed God. They let Satan and his lies bring sin into the garden. By introducing sin, nothing has ever been the same between God and man. Disobeying God has consequences, then and now.

From the sins of the past, the present, and the future, people don't understand that Christ's return is at hand and near. Pride, arrogance, greed, and self-centeredness have been the driving force of men since Adam and Eve abandoned God and His holiness. In the beginning, man was in an exceptional relationship with God. When Satan entered the picture and lied to Eve, and she convinced Adam, they turned away from God's love. Adam and Eve believed the lies that Satan told them. Satan is still telling those lies, and man is still believing what Satan is saying. Satan's greatest deception tool is repetition. If you tell a lie long enough, people believe the lie over the truth. Anything and everything that Satan touches is evil and causes great pain.

From the start of time until the end of time, Christ will have arrived on earth twice. Christ's impact on the people of this world was and is and will be great.

Christ First Coming

Jesus came to earth. He was flesh and blood and walked among us. He was born of a virgin and lived a sin free life. Christ died on the cross; raised from the dead; and lives today with God, the Father in heaven. He is the Savior of humanity. Jesus died to save you and me from our sins. He paid the price for all.

Jesus brought peace, an inner peace, to a world in tribulation. Man was in true form, in the way he poured out cruelty on his fellow man. No longer would man need to bring an animal to sacrifice and shed its blood to pay for their sins. Christ's blood and sacrifice took care of that. God made a way, and Christ is that way. Christ intercedes on our behalf.

Mary was betrothed to Joseph. Before they came together, Mary became pregnant. Joseph was thinking about putting Mary away secretly. While he was thinking about doing this, an angel came to him in a dream and said, "Don't be afraid to make Mary your wife. What was conceived in Mary was of the Holy Spirit, and she will have a son, and you shall call him Jesus. He will save his people from their sins. This would fulfill what a prophet said, 'Behold the virgin shall be with child, and bear a Son, and they shall call His name Immanuel,' this means, 'God with us.'" Reference to Matthew 1:18–23.

When Christ arrived, it was to accomplish two things: bring peace (spiritual, not physical) and to become the sacrifice for our sins. Christ is the mediator between God and man. Jesus has access to God the Father. He is the only one capable of crossing the gap between God and man.

Christ's Second Coming

Christ will return one day to call the chosen and faithful to be with Him. Every man, woman, and child will see Him at His return. All who stay the course and remain faithful to the end, Christ will come for them, and they will meet Him in the clouds. The dead will rise first, then the ones still following His leading here on earth will be next to join Christ in the air. From that moment on, we will be with Christ forever. Amen!

> But I do not want you to be ignorant, brethren, concerning those who have fallen asleep, least you sorrow as others who have no hope. For if we believe that Jesus died and rose again, even so God will bring with Him those who sleep in Jesus.
>
> For this we say to you by the word of the Lord, that we who are alive and remain until the coming of the Lord will by no means proceed those who are asleep. For the Lord Himself will descend from heaven with a shout, with the voice of an archangel, and with the trumpet of God. And the dead in Christ will rise first. Then we who are alive and remain shall be caught up together with them in the clouds to meet the Lord in the air. And thus we shall always be with the Lord. Therefore comfort one another with these words. (1 Thess. 4:13–18 NKJV)

His second coming will be when He returns for the chosen and the faithful. The chosen are the Jews who believe in Christ, and the faithful is His church (saints). His coming will be for the believers who overcome and preserve until the end. They will join Him in the air at His return.

CHAPTER 5

Important Reading

REMEMBER, GOD CREATED THE UNIVERSE, heaven, and earth. God created man, He said, "Let us create man in our image." That makes man different from everything else. God desires to have fellowship with man on a different level than with the angels. When you read God's word, you see the enormous love He has for what He created: man. God knew this was something special. He placed His creation in a garden. This garden was a place where man could exist and have fellowship with God.

When you read the Word of God, you see the way He cares for humanity. This explains the extent to which God's involvement is with man. It shows how people have become what they are today and what they will be in the future. Men have chosen not to obey God but to sin. God's plan is to make a way to restore man to a right relationship to Himself. God made men with a will because He desires to fellowship with someone who thinks and can make decisions. He created everything and has everything, so why make man with a choice? God wants fellowship with a being who chooses to fellowship, worship, and love Him for who He is. He desires a relationship with men, and He wants true fellowship. The problem came when man sinned and disobeyed God, and disobedience to God is sin. God will not rationalize sin away. As you read the Bible, you see how God deals with a sinful and rebellious people.

The first book in the Bible is Genesis, and you will see what an extraordinary book the Bible is to read as you look at an overview of Genesis. The Bible explains so much about men. It reveals our purpose. Yes, there is a purpose for man on earth. That purpose is to have fellowship and worship God! The Bible shows man's fellowship with God, and it shows man's fall from grace. God's plan is to save men from their sin that enslaves them. Sin separates man from God.

Genesis

The first book in the Bible starts with creation. How men and women came to be on this planet. It was not an accident, or some random whim of a superpower being, or by someone bored of what was happening around Him. It was intentional of a loving God who wanted fellowship with His creation.

"In the beginning God created the heavens and the earth" (Gen. 1:1 NKJV).

Day 1: God made light. The light He called day and the darkness He called night.
Day 2: God divided the waters above and below the firmament.
Day 3: God created the land, the sea, and the plant life.
Day 4: God created the sun and the moon and the stars and made them visible.
Day 5: God made every living creature in the seas and every living winged creature that flies. God said, "Let them be fruitful and multiply."
Day 6: God created every living creature on land, and all things that exist. God made man and woman and empowered them over all living creatures.
Day 7: God rested.

God looked at all that He had done and was pleased. The water above and below the firmament would have created a unique atmosphere. This was a tropical environment, and this helps explain the long life span that people had. He is the creator of everything. All things are possible with God. Our limitations are not His.

God created man from the dust of the ground. He breathed into him the breath of life. When God created man, He created a garden for him and put everything that man would need in this garden. God put man in the garden to tend and keep it. This shows that man shouldn't say idle. Man needs to work and look after what God put here for him. There were rules that Adam had to obey.

> And the Lord God commanded the man, saying, "Of every tree of the garden you may freely eat; but of the tree of knowledge of good and evil you shall not eat, for in the day that you eat of it you shall surely die." (Gen. 2:16–17 NKJV)

God said, "It is not good for man to be alone. I will make him a helper." When God made this helper, He took one of Adam's ribs. God brought this helper to Adam, and he called her woman.

> And Adam said: "This is now bone of my bones and flesh of my flesh; she shall be called Woman, because she was taken out of Man." (Gen. 2:23 NKJV)

God reveals His greatness to us in so many ways, and it's just astonishing when you see glimpses of His majesty. In the first marriage, God institutes and ordained this union between husband and wife. God was, and is, telling us what makes up a good marriage. Man does his best to change what God tells us from time to time and makes it seem right. From the beginning, one man and one woman make an appropriate marriage.

Adam and Eve were tested, and they failed. The serpent convinced Eve, and she disobeyed. Eve convinced Adam, and he disobeyed. Then one evening God came to walk through the garden as He had done before. This time was different! Sin had entered the picture now. They chose to disobey what the Lord had forbidden them to do. This knowledge of good and evil was not what they believed it would be. *It never is.* Sin is never what it appears to be at first. Sin always looks glamorous and wonderful at first. The result is always the same, terrible, because it causes separation between man and God. They hid from God because now they knew they were naked. It wouldn't be the last time Adam and Eve would experience fear. They didn't know what God would do to them when He found out that they were disobedient to Him.

For every sin, there is a consequence. God would punish the snake (Satan), the woman (Eve), and the man (Adam) for each part in the disobedience of their sin. Snake's punishment is to move on its belly the rest of its existence. Woman's punishment would be too have pain in childbirth. Man's punishment would be to toil the ground for his food and would have hardship in doing so. God is a just God. He will not tolerate sin. God clothed Adam and Eve to provide for their nakedness. They could care for each other and establish a family where God placed them. God sent them to a land outside the garden of Eden. This way they could not eat from the tree of life. God provided for them even though they didn't do what God ask them to do. This act of disobedience would not be the last time man would not keep his word with God.

There were two sons of Adam and Eve, and their names were Cain and Abel. They both brought an offering to the Lord. Abe's offering, God accepted, and Cain's offering, God did not. This made Cain so angry that he set out to kill his brother, and he did just that. Cain's sin was not in what he brought to the Lord but the attitude of his heart that the Lord didn't like. God punished Cain for killing his brother and the sin in his heart. The Lord gave them another son. His name was Seth.

> After he begot Seth, the days of Adam were eight hundred years; and he had sons and daughters.
> (Gen. 5:4 NKJV)

IMPORTANT READING

From the time of Adam to the time of Noah, man's numbers grew, and his sins also multiplied. People have become so evil, so self-indulgent, that men found new horrible ways to disobey God. Man was finding more pleasure in his self-centeredness than being with God. When man stopped turning to God, God was so disappointed in man that He regretted making him. God decided that He would destroy man, and everything living on the earth, with a great flood. God noticed one man and took favor on him, and his name was Noah. The Lord instructed Noah to build an ark. Because of Noah's obedience, there would be a remnant of creation surviving the great flood. Nothing survived but what God put on the ark, the ark that Noah built. Noah received the plans and instructions for the ark and constructed it as God designed it. Just like the ark, if we follow God's word, things will always work out. Noah did what God instructed him to do. God has a plan for each of us. If only we would surrender our control to Him—His miracles, His mercy, and His love—they will flow through each of us and touch the lives of others around us.

Reading about the inhabitants in Noah's time, we see the purpose of the Lord in judgment and the purpose of the Lord in grace. Because of the sins of the people who were on earth, God punish them and everything that lived on dry land. The sin of man was so great that God couldn't look the other way and let it go. God gave His grace to Noah and his family and two of every kind of animal. When all of Noah and his family and two of every kind of animal were on the ark, God shut the door, and the rain began. So much water fell from heaven that the water covered the entire earth. No living thing that breathed on dry land survived except what was on the ark.

The waters of the great flood that cover the earth started to subside. As the waters disappeared, the ark came to rest on land. Noah and his family emerged from the ark and thanked God for saving their lives. God established His covenant with Noah: never again shall He destroy all flesh with the waters of a flood. We can see God's promise today in the many colors of the rainbow after the rain. All the people of all the nations descend from Adam, and then from Noah.

The failure of people at Babel: men built a city that would reach to the heavens. Man's speech was a single language. They could work and communicate with one another to accomplish anything. God confused their speech so they could not communicate with each other because of what men were attempting. God moved people all over the world to slow down the spread of evil.

Seth descended from Terah and was Abram's father. Abram was born 2176 BC.

> Now the Lord had said to Abram: "Get out of your country, from your family and from your father's house, to a land that I will show you. I will make you a great nation; I will bless you and make your name great; and you shall be a blessing. I will bless those who bless you, and I will curse him who curses you; and in you all the families of the earth shall be blessed." (Gen. 12:1–3 NKJV)

Abram received a promise from God. He worshiped God and had communion with Him. Abram was human, and he made mistakes, just as any individual does. Our faith versus our fears: which one will we choose to give control over our lives? Abram chose faith, not knowing where the Lord was sending him, but he went.

We build character in times of struggle, hardship, and trials. It's not a matter of whether trouble will come, because it will show up. Will we listen to Satan who lies or to God who is truth? The question is not will Satan try to deceive us but when? Fear can be healthy, and it can be unhealthy.

Abram entered the land of Egypt and became afraid that the Egyptians would kill him and take his wife. She was a beautiful woman. Abram told them she was his sister. The Egyptians took her. God caused a plague on Pharaoh and his family until he returned Sarai to Abram. Abram and Lot had to leave Egypt.

IMPORTANT READING

When Abram and Lot left Egypt, they entered Canaan, but the land could not support the both of them. Abram gave Lot the choice which place he would live: the mountains or the rich, plush valley. Lot chose the valley. This was a garden environment. Lot pitched his tents next to a large city in the valley, Sodom. God came to Abram, high on a mountain, and told him, "I give you all you can see north, west, south, and east. This land will be yours, and your descendants, forever."

In the next few years, Lot and his family became a prisoner by invaders. This army captured them and fled toward a land far away. When Abram heard of this, he gathered all his workers and went after his brother. Abram and his men did battle and took his brother, his family, and all his things back. God was with Abram. God is El Elyon, meaning the most high, possessor of heaven and earth.

God confirmed His covenant with Abram, and from Abram's body, his descendants will multiply. Sarai rationalized in her mind that she was getting beyond childbearing years and didn't want to wait on the Lord to fulfill His word. So Sarai schemed to give her handmaid to Abram to carry on the family line. The handmaid's name was Hagar, and when she became pregnant, she looked at Sarai differently. Hagar had a boy and named him Ishmael. Sarai dealt with Hagar harshly after the birth of Ishmael. God told Sarai that He would bless her child, and his name was to be Isaac. The Lord will also bless Ishmael, and he will become a nation.

God changed Abram's name to Abraham. Abraham means "the friend of God." There were two cities next to one another, Sodom and Gomorrah. They had become so evil, doing all kinds of evil against man and God. Abraham was an intercessor for Sodom. He pleaded with God not to destroy the righteous men with the evil men of Sodom. God sent angels to Sodom to find righteous men like Abraham pleaded. Lot would sacrifice his daughters to the immoral men of Sodom rather than have them abuse and harm the angels. Sodom's sin was so great that the angels told Lot to get his family out of Sodom, and none of them were to look back as they were leaving. "If any of you look back, you will die." Traveling over the mountain, Lot's wife looked back as they were leaving the area, and

God changed her into a pillar of salt. God destroyed Sodom and Gomorrah because of the gross, perverse, evil sin that was taking place.

The daughters of Lot feared that their family lineage would stop. Lot's girls got their father drunk with wine and slept with him. Lot did not know what was happening. Both daughters became pregnant: one, the father of the Moabites today, and the other one, the father of the Ammon until now.

God instructed Abraham to change the name Sarai to Sarah. The Lord blesses Abraham and Sarah with a baby, and Abraham called his son Isaac. When Isaac was born, Sarah demanded Hagar and Ishmael go. Hagar was Sarah's handmaid and could do as she wanted with her, so Abraham sent them away.

God tested Abraham's faith. God told Abraham to take Isaac as an offering. Abraham acted as the Lord said and took Isaac and prepared to sacrifice him. God let the sacrifice go to a point, and when He knew Abraham would not keep even his child from Him, He supplied the sacrifice. God wanted to see action, not just words. Abraham did not withhold his boy from God.

> God said, "Blessing I will bless you, and multiplying I will multiply your descendants as the stars of the heaven and as the sand which is on the seashore; and your descendants shall possess the gates of their enemies. In your seed all nations of the earth shall be blessed, because you have obeyed My voice." (Gen. 22:17–18 NKJV)

Abraham and his family were in a foreign country when Sarah died. Abraham purchased a cave to bury Sarah, a plot in the field of Machpelah, in the land of Canaan.

Abraham sent a servant back to his father's house in search of a bride for his son, Isaac. He prayed that he would know the right woman for Isaac. God provided, and Rebekah was the name of Isaac's wife. When Abraham passed away, Isaac had him buried next to his mother. God blessed Isaac, the heir of God's promise to Abraham.

IMPORTANT READING

Isaac and Rebekah had two sons, and their names were Esau and Jacob. Esau was the firstborn, and Jacob was the second. Esau sells his birthright to Jacob for food. When Isaac was old, his vision was failing. Before Isaac goes to be with the Lord, he needed to bless the firstborn. Rebekah and Jacob set out to steal Esau's blessing. Rebekah made Isaac the meal that Esau was to bring before Isaac. Jacob took the meal in and lied to Isaac and told him he was Esau. Isaac blessed Jacob instead of Esau. When Esau returned, Isaac had no more blessing to give. When Isaac couldn't bless Esau, he set out to murder Jacob. Rebekah heard Esau was planning to kill Jacob. She had him go live with her brother, Laban. While Jacob was away, Esau marries Mahalath, a daughter of a Canaanite. Jacob had a dream on his way to his uncle's house. In this dream, Jacob saw a ladder going up to heaven.

> And behold, the Lord stood above it and said: "I am the Lord God of Abraham your father and the God of Isaac; the land on which you lie I will give to you and your descendants. Also your descendants shall be as the dust of the earth; you shall spread aboard to the West and to the East, to the North and to the South; and in you and your seed all families of the earth shall be blessed. Behold, I am with you and will keep you wherever you go, and will bring you back to this land; for I will not leave you until I have done what I have spoken to you." (Gen. 28:13–15 NKJV)

Jacob named this place Bethel.

> Then Jacob made a vow, saying, "If God will be with me, and keep me in this way that I am going, and give me bread to eat and clothing to put on, so that I come back to my father's house in peace, then the Lord shall be my God." (Gen. 28:20–21 NKJV)

IS THERE TIME

Jacob reaches Haran. Jacob makes an agreement with Laban, his mother's brother. The agreement is to work seven years for no wages to marry Rachel, Laban's daughter. At the end of the seven years, Jacob marries. In the morning, when Jacob awoke, he discovered that Laban had tricked him. He had married Leah, Rachel's sister. Jacob confronted Laban, and Laban told him that no one marries the younger before the older daughter was married. Laban said, "If you serve me another seven years, I'll give you Rachel." Jacob agreed to work another seven years for Rachel. Jacob married Rachel at the end of the second seven years of free service.

Jacob fled from Laban because he knew Laban would not let him go with what was his. Jacob left without Laban knowing. Laban pursues Jacob because he feared that Jacob's God would destroy him because of the way he deceived Jacob. Jacob made a covenant with Laban.

> This heap is a witness, and this pillar is a witness, that I will not pass beyond this heap to you, and you will not pass beyond this heap and this pillar to me, for harm. (Gen. 31:52 NKJV)

In the morning, Laban said his goodbyes to his children and grandchildren and returns home. Jacob prepares to see Esau. Esau hears of Jacob's return and goes out to his brother.

On the way, Jacob wrestles with God.

> And He said, "Your name shall no longer be called Jacob, but Israel; for you have struggled with God and with men, and have prevailed." (Gen. 32:28 NKJV)

The name Jacob means supplanter. Supplanter means to supersede another by force or treachery. The name Israel means or suggests royalty, power, and sovereignty among men. When Jacob yielded, he became a new man, God-led. The name Israel would be the reference to the new nation. Israel is the name of the father of the twelve sons of Jacob. The twelve sons of Jacob are the twelve tribes of Israel. The descendants of Jacob are the nation of Israel today.

Jacob humbles himself and prepares to ask forgiveness from his brother. Esau is pleased to see his brother. They embraced with joy, and the families were reunited. Jacob worshiped God and erected an altar and called it El Elohe Israel. This was an act of faith. El Elohe Israel, the title given by Jacob to a spot that was consecrated ground. The Almighty God, He is powerful and strong. The one true God, Emmanuel: God is with us. He is the God of our salvation, a loving God. It conveys in scripture that God is the Creator, King, Judge, Lord, and Savior. His character is compassionate, gracious, and faithful to His followers.

A young prince in the area that Jacob and his household were living found Jacob's daughter beautiful, and her charm consumed him. The prince desired her, so he took her and defiled her. The prince came and informed the family that he wanted to marry her. Jacob's sons devised a plan to sin. They set out to get revenge for the wrong done to their sister. They told the king and the prince that the only way he could have Dinah is to become circumcised. The king and the prince agreed all the men of their kingdom would comply. On the third day, they were in great pain and could hardly move. Two of Jacob's sons came with a sword and killed every man. There was no male left alive in that kingdom; and they took Dinah, their sister, back. After this sin, Jacob, all his family, herds, and servants moved to Bethel. Jacob restored communion with God there.

Jacob and Rachel had two boys, Joseph and Benjamin. Rachel died giving childbirth to Benjamin. The sons of Jacob were Reuben, Simon, Levi, Judah, Issachar, Zebulun, Joseph, Benjamin, Dan, Naphtali, Gad, and Asher. These are the twelve tribes of Israel. After Jacob returned to the family, Isaac passed on. Jacob and Esau buried their father. Esau was the father of the Edomites and lived in Mount Seir, the land of Edom. Esau had many descendants.

Joseph was Jacob's favorite child, and it was apparent how Jacob felt about Joseph compared to the others. They could see the special attention that Jacob was paying to Joseph, and they hated him for it. One night, Joseph had a dream in which he would stand above his brothers and they would bow down to him. This created a divide between them. They hated him much more for the dream of having to submit to their younger brother, whom they disliked already. Jacob made a coat of many colors for Joseph. When Joseph put on the coat, he stood out. This was like rubbing salt in a festering wound. One day, Jacob had Joseph go out and check on his brothers. They saw Joseph coming at a distance. They just couldn't stand it anymore. They cast him into a pit to die. They changed their minds and sold him to a trader passing by. The caravan of these traders were going to Egypt. That way Joseph's brothers would never have to see him ever again. They slew an animal and rubbed its blood into the coat of many colors. They took the coat back to Jacob. The brothers told Jacob that they had discovered the coat and that a beast must have killed Joseph because there was no sign of him. Jacob mourned for the death of his beloved son, Joseph.

When Joseph arrived in Egypt, a man named Potiphar was at the market that day. The traders sold their slaves, and Potiphar purchased Joseph. Joseph became Potiphar's slave and served him on his land. All things that Joseph did and touched, the Lord prospered. The Lord blessed Joseph's dealings and that pleased Potiphar. One day, when Potiphar was elsewhere, his wife wanted to have a relationship with Joseph, the kind of relationship that a husband and wife only have. Joseph would have nothing to do with it because Joseph was an honorable man. This infuriates her, and she makes up a story that the manservant, Joseph, took advantage of her while Potiphar was away. When Potiphar returned, he sent Joseph to prison for a crime he didn't commit.

No one appeared to be thinking of Joseph in jail. Pharaoh sent his chief butler and baker to the same prison. The butler and the baker both had a dream, and Joseph interpreted their dreams for them. The events occurred as Joseph said. One would die, and the other would return to their place of service in Pharaoh's palace.

Pharaoh had a dream, and there was no one who could explain it. The dream troubled Pharaoh. Pharaoh was worried and wanted to find out what the dream meant. The butler, who had a dream in prison, remembered Joseph as being able to interpret his dream.

IMPORTANT READING

He told the Pharaoh about it, and the Pharaoh sent for Joseph. The Pharaoh wanted to see if Joseph could explain his dream. Joseph explained the dream, and Pharaoh believed him. Joseph came into power, and God made it happen. Pharaoh gave Joseph the authority to prepare the land for what lay ahead. Only the Pharaoh had more power than Joseph in Egypt. Joseph prepared Egypt for the great famine that was about to take place.

The great famine was rampant. Great hunger was hitting everywhere and was afflicting everyone. This great famine began to take its toll upon Jacob and his sons. They needed food. The famine was bad, the starvation ran throughout the known world, and Jacob was hoping that the food could get his family through this hard time. Everyone from the known world was going to Egypt for food. All food coming out of Egypt had to go through Joseph. Jacob and all his family were running out of food, and the famine was getting worse. Jacob sent his sons to get food from Egypt. Jacob didn't send Benjamin. Joseph saw his brothers and tested them. His brothers did not recognize who Joseph was. Joseph set them up and accused them of stealing from Pharaoh. They denied doing any such thing. They claimed to be honorable men. Joseph told them, "One of you will remain here, and the others will bring your youngest brother here, and that will prove you are innocent." Simon stayed while the others returned home to get Benjamin. This was to prove their innocence to the man in charge of Egypt. And Jacob answered, "No! Benjamin will not go, they will kill him." Jacob couldn't live if something were to happen to Benjamin. The famine was getting worse. The food was running out, and Jacob had no choice but to let Benjamin travel to Egypt. They went to Egypt for Simon and more food. Judah told his father, "If I do not bring Benjamin back to you, let the burden fall on me." Benjamin and his brothers returned to Egypt as Joseph had requested. They brought some of the finest things from their area and doubled the money. This was to convince the man in charge that they were honest people in hopes he would sell them food.

Joseph's brothers arrived in Egypt, and Joseph entertained them. While they were eating, Joseph's cup became missing. And Joseph told them that whoever took the cup, they will perish. They searched the bags and found it in Benjamin's bag. Judah stepped forward and said, "I will take Benjamin's place. If Benjamin were to die, it would kill our father." Joseph could no longer contain himself and revealed himself to them. The brothers were in shock and surprised. Joseph sent his brothers back to bring Jacob and the family to Egypt.

With Joseph next in command in Egypt, his family would not have to worry about the famine. Jacob and his family traveled to Egypt and settled in Goshen. Joseph promised to bury Jacob in the field that Abraham had purchased in Canaan when he passed. Jacob blessed all of Joseph's children according to his blessing. When he was finished with the blessings, he breathed his last breath. Joseph buried his father where Jacob had requested. When Jacob died, Joseph's brothers became frightened for their lives. Joseph reassures them that as long as he was alive, they had nothing to fear. God had blessed him, and everything worked out to God's plan.

> Then Joseph took an oath from the children of Israel, saying, "God will surely visit you, and you shall carry my bones from here." (Gen. 50:25 NKJV)

Moses wrote Genesis to encourage the Israelites, to explain why their ancestors went to Egypt, and why they had a promise land besides Egypt.

There are four concepts that are necessary for understanding the Bible:

- God worked in the lives of Abraham and Sarah and is the God who created the universe. He is the only one true and living God, the Creator, and Savior of the world. He was the same then and the same now.
- Humanity has inherited a state of sinfulness from Adam and Eve. Adam and Eve sinned in the garden. All people rebel against God.
- God offers forgiveness but judges and will continue to judge the actions of every man and woman. God made it

IMPORTANT READING

clear by the flood in Noah's time and by the sin of Sodom and Gomorrah that he would not tolerate sin. Human wickedness is unacceptable to God. God cannot let evil go unpunished.
- Sin continues to plague all of humanity. God has a plan to save humanity from man's evil deeds.

God's plan is Jesus Christ!

CHAPTER 6

People Look at Things Differently

WE ARE A UNIQUE CREATURE on this planet. There is nothing quite like us in this world. Either we don't belong with all the other creatures, or someone placed us here to exist among them. We are a very diverse being. Humans come from many lifestyles. People look at things differently from one country to the next. Our traditions are what set us apart. Humanity is complex.

Adam and Eve committed the first sin; it set the stage for our differences. The differences separate us from each other in ways we are still learning about. We have developed into several kinds of people: caring, loving, self-centered, hateful, wicked, and provoking. Our culture that we come from makes us all different from each other. That in its self is not a bad thing. Our differences make us unique. So with all these diversities, how do we all get along with each other? There is one common denominator that can cross all the differences that the world comes up with: that is Jesus Christ.

Humans must have rules and guidelines to live by. We need limits to stay focused on what is right. One of the most important rules God gave to man, and he didn't keep it. We are to show love to others.

IS THERE TIME

A man asks Jesus, what is the most important commandment? Jesus answered him,

> The first of all the commandments is: "Hear, O Israel, the Lord our God, the Lord is one. And you shall love the Lord your God with all your heart, with all your soul, with all your mind, and with all your strength." This is the first commandment. And the second, like it, is this: "You shall love your neighbor as yourself." There is no other commandment greater than these. (Mark 12:29–30 NKJV)

If man could live by these two commandments,
the world would be in a much better state.

Look at the different denominations. Most of them can't even agree on what to believe, how to act. They seem to invent the rules that they follow. There was a guide that was given to us to use, and that guide is the Bible. Rules show us how to worship, baptize, and have communion with God. All our denominations, our rules, our regulations remind me of a group of individuals in the Bible: the Pharisees, the Sadducees, and the scribes. They established rules just too have rules to keep people in line with their way of thinking, not God's. By trying to keep all the rules and regulations they made up, they missed the part about fellowship with God. The reason God made us in the first place is to fellowship with Him. If you doubt that, look at the first people ever created by God, Adam and Eve. What was the main thing they were supposed to do? They were to fellowship with God. Individuals started making up so many rules. Instead of the rules and regulations being a way to God, they became their god. Do the rules and regulations in the congregation you attend make it a path to find God or do they seem to hinder the process? Is Christ the focus of the congregation, or is accomplishing all the different tasks the focus? In the congregation you attend, are the staff and the programs the focus or is sharing Christ? Christ should and must be the focus of everything we do as a congregation. Remember, the church is the bride of Christ, and the church is the people, not the building. The building is just a place where the church meets.

If we look back in time, everyone spoke one language. One person could communicate with any other person. God changed this because as man could talk with everyone in one language, evil spread and sin became worse. God slowed down man's sin because evil was getting worse. How many languages can a person speak and understand? The more we communicate and learn each other's language on this planet, the more sin seems to spread and be out in the open. Right becomes wrong, and wrong becomes right. Humans convince themselves that they don't need God. Man thinks he can do anything and says look at what I have done. He loses sight of something important. God made everything. Man made nothing on his own. It is all from God.

God created us to have fellowship with Him. God wants fellowship with man. He cannot and will not tolerate sin. The world would want us to believe that we need to be more tolerant. God will not rationalize sin to be acceptable. Satan is the master of deception, making sin look right. Sin is never right, only appears to be right for a short time. If we remove our eyes from God, we deceive ourselves, and Satan will convince us into thinking we are serving God, but it is Satan. His deception is great. Even the strongest of men, when they look away from God, will fall. In man's strength, Satan will win. In God's strength, Satan doesn't stand a chance.

What should concern Christians today? Could legislation pass that makes speaking or writing what the Bible reveals to be sin to become a hate crime. Christians will have to decide one day, will they stand up for what the Bible says or bow to the new bible that is coming? Christians will need to know the Bible, the Bible as it is. The ones in power will want it changed? It's interesting to look at a version of the Bible and compare it with one ten, twenty years ago. It might surprise you. Some changes make it easier to understand; but some changes, even one word, can change the meaning. Be careful because the changes will be subtle at first. The powers to be will do away with parts of the Bible if it doesn't fit their agenda. Christians must put God's word into their minds. They have to know the Bible so well they don't need the printed word to share with someone. I believe this will be essential one day.

If the powers to be change the Bible, will Christians relinquish the Bibles that they have had for centuries? Will they accept the new version? Use the more worldly language, one more tolerant and accepting of everyone's view, one that is without all of God's word? Will we stand for God and what we believe? Could we become the outlaw viewed as a troublemaker in society? Can the government empower a homeland security force that has as much power as the military and with good funding? What will that mean to Christians? What brand of justice will Christians have to endure? Someday, Christians standing up for what they believe in and what the Bible says will make the news and be viewed as the outlaw. It will become a realty one day. When you're on trial for being a Christian, will there be enough evidence to convict you?

For security, governments will need a way of identifying who you are and where you are. They have the technology to put this small chip on the back of your hand or on your forehead. This chip will contain all your information to protect you. But is it to protect you? If you are in trouble, they will know right where to find you, for your protection. Anyone not taking this chip will have problems with the government. For security and your protection, only the ones who carry the identifying mark will be able to buy and sell anything. Remember, they will tell you it's for your security and protection.

> He causes all, both small and great, rich and poor, free and slave, to receive a mark on their right hand or on their foreheads, and that no one may buy or sell except one who has the mark or the name of the beast, or the number of his name. (Rev. 13:16–17 NKJV)

The number of the beast is 666.

PEOPLE LOOK AT THINGS DIFFERENTLY

How many individuals have put markings all over themselves? It's an accepted practice that people are becoming more and more comfortable with. Almost everyone knows someone, a family member, a friend, a coworker who has a mark on their body some place. Is Satan conditioning us to accept marks on our bodies to be acceptable?

CHAPTER 7

Sexual Immorality

SEXUAL IMMORALITY CAN BE MANY things. Some of the best words to describe sexual immorality would be *pornography, fornication, an immoral act, any practice involving sex outside of marriage.* The proper place for sex is between one man and one woman inside of marriage. The definition of marriage is a person of the opposite sex as husband or wife, one man and one woman. Consensual sex, intercourse between two persons not married to each other as set down by God, is sin. God gave us an example of what marriage should be, Adam and Eve, one man and one woman. Scripture describes sexual immorality as sinful behavior.

This chapter on sexual immorality has so many important things to understand how God looks at sexual immorality. How humans, men and women, should deal with this desire (sex drive) that we have. This sex drive can build a bond between a man and a woman when they become one. Marriage is the only acceptable place for sex. If this sex drive in man or woman gets out of control, it will destroy the man or the woman, or both. Marriage will not survive when sexual immorality exists within it.

IS THERE TIME

> For this is the will of God, your sanctification:
> that you should abstain from sexual immorality.
> (1 Thess. 4:3 NKJV)

> Sanctification means to set apart for special
> use or purpose, to make holy.

One way to define sexual immorality is a moment of pleasure, and when the moment of pleasure passes, there is a lifetime of pain. What is sexual immorality? Sexual immorality is any illicit sexual activity outside of marriage. God designed marriage to unify and strengthen man and woman. The unification will fulfill each other and also this is how we reproduce and have offspring. Sanctification, the state of growing in divine grace and the commitment after conversion of the Christian. Scripture prohibits sexual activity of *adultery, bestiality, homosexuality, lust,* or *incest*. Another term used in Revelation is *whoremonger* in the King James Version. Whoremonger is a person who spreads something that is discreditable, a man or woman who engages in sexual acts for money, an immoral man or woman.

The Bible puts sexually immoral people in some evil company. God let men with this debased mind do things that are not acceptable to God. They are filled with what is unfitting to God:

unrighteousness	sexual immorality	wickedness
covetousness	maliciousness	full of envy
murder	strife	deceit
evil-mindedness	whispers	backbiters
haters of God	violent	proud
boasters	inventors of evil things	disobedient to parents
undiscerning	untrustworthy	unloving
unforgiving	unmerciful	

They know the righteous judgments of God. They practice these things anyway. According to God, these are deserving of death. Reference to Romans 1:28–32.

SEXUAL IMMORALITY

Debase: reduce the moral character of a person

The book of Revelation reveals who will be cast into Satan's eternal place, which is the lake of fire. All who go there will be tormented with Satan, forever. This is one group of people you definitely don't want to be a part of. God spells out who will have to go to the lake of fire and who will not. This is a place of separation from God forever:

Everyone that overcomes shall have all things, and I will be His God, and he will be with Me.

But cowardly, unbelieving, abominable, murders, sexually immoral, sorcerers, idolaters, all liars, will be in the lake of fire, which is the second death. Reference to Revelation 21:7–8.

Cowardly: lacking in courage, timid and fainthearted
Unbelieving: rejecting any belief in God, denying religion, and knowledge of spiritual matters
Abominable: unequivocally detestable, exceptionally bad or displeasing
Murder: kill intentionally and with premeditation
Sexual immorality: adultery, bestiality, homosexuality, lust, incest, pornography, fornication, an immoral act, any practice involving sex outside of marriage. Acceptable marriage is between one man and one woman.
Sorcerers: one who practices magic or evil spells
Idolaters: a person who worships idols
Liars: a person who doesn't tell the truth

Different versions of the Bible use different terms when describing these things.

Example:

Revelation 2:21
"And I gave her time to repent of her *sexual immorality*, and she did not repent (NKJV).

"And I gave her space to repent of her *fornication*; and she repented not (KJV).

IS THERE TIME

"I have given her time to repent of her *immorality*, but she is unwilling (NIV).

Revelation Verses:

New King James Version		King James Version			New International Version		
Adulteries	Sexual Immorality	Sexually Immoral	Fornication	Woremongers	Sexual Immorality	Immorality	Adultery
2:14	21:18	14:8	2:14	17:2	2:14	2:21	17:2
14:8				21:8			
2:20	22:15	17:2	2:20	17:4	2:20		18:9
17:4				22:15			
2:21		17:4	2:21	18:3	9:21		
18:3							
9:21		18:3	9:21	18:9	21:8		
19:2							
		19:2	14:8	19:2	22:15		

Adultery is sex outside of marriage. When a man or a woman, who is married, has sex outside of his or her marriage, this action is adultery. It is called an affair. This is sin. God intended for us to stay faithful to the partner that we made that vow to on our wedding day, the one we consummated with on our wedding night. Sex has no place outside of marriage, *period*! God's design for sex is only between one man and one woman in marriage. Marriage is not about one moment of pleasure or infatuation that comes when we first are getting to know a person. It's about a commitment to our mate for as long as we both live. Sex is one of the strengthening aspects of marriage.

According to Scripture, adultery is forbidden. Adultery destroys the marriage and the family. It shatters the very foundation of marriage, the trust. It robs marriage of a proper biblical way of life. The Ten Commandments is very explicit about adultery. The seriousness of this sin, and whether we should partake of it, is clear in the Bible. It is a mistake to practice this sin in our life. If you choose this behavior, *you are making a conscious decision to sin*, and Satan has deceived you.

"You shall not commit adultery" (Exod. 20:14 NKJV). Now you have to admit, that's clear.

> The man who commits adultery with another man's wife, he who commits adultery with his neighbor's wife, the adulterer and the adulteress, shall be put to death. (Lev. 20:10 NKJV)

The Old Testament contained no toleration for adultery. If you committed adultery, the man and the woman who committed it were to be put to death. The Proverbs states that adultery destroys the soul of the perpetrator.

> Whoever commits adultery with a woman lacks understanding; he who does so destroys his own soul. (Prov. 6:32 NKJV)

In the New Testament, Jesus gives counsel to the rich young ruler.

> Now behold, one came and said to Him, "Good Teacher, what good thing shall I do that I may have eternal life?" So He said to him, "Why do you call Me good? No one is good but One, that is, God. But if you want to enter into life, keep the commandments." He said to Him, "Which ones?" Jesus said, "You shall not murder. You shall not commit adultery. You shall not steal. You shall not bear false witness. Honor your father and your mother. You shall love your neighbor as yourself." (Matt. 19:16–19 NKJV)

There are four things on the list of things not to do and two things to do. You shall not commit adultery is on the list of things not to do.

This sin is one of those sins man rationalizes, not so bad with little or no consequences. Men don't hold people accountable for their actions (sins). Man's view of this sin is, it's okay, everybody's doing it. In reality, everyone is *not* doing it. It just appears to be that way, to prey on the weak. God's word is clear: adultery is a sin. In man's view, it can be rationalized to be acceptable. Man's outlook is don't worry about it. Our TVs keep pounding it into what we hear every day. All is okay when in fact everything is not okay. In God's view, sin is sin. There is no rationalizing to it!

To lose control of your desires and let them control you have always had harsh consequences. Too many times in the evolution of man, man rationalizes sin into an acceptable way of life. Sin is never an acceptable way of life, and it always destroys everything it touches.

Bestiality is sex with an animal. The Bible prohibits this deviant behavior. If you choose this behavior, *you are making a conscious decision to sin.*

> Whoever lies with an animal shall surely be put to death. (Exod. 22:19 NKJV)

> Nor shall you mate with any animal, to defile yourself with it. Nor shall any woman stand before an animal to mate with it. It is a perversion. (Lev. 18:23 NKJV)

> If a man mates with an animal, he shall surely be put to death, and you shall kill the animal. If a woman approaches any animal and mates with it, you shall kill the woman and the animal. They shall surely be put to death. Their blood is upon them. (Lev. 20:15–16 NKJV)

SEXUAL IMMORALITY

This is an unnatural act, for a man or a woman, to have sex with an animal. God's design for sex in humans is to be between a man and a woman in marriage. Sex is a beautiful thing. Sex is one of God's gifts to us, a way to reproduce and a way to unite man and woman with a bond that strengthens the two as they become one.

Homosexuality is sex with a person of the same sex (man with man or woman with woman). The Old and New Testament condemn sex with the same-sex individual. The act of homosexuality is not a right; it is a sin. Homosexuality is *not* something you are born with. If you choose this behavior, *you are making a conscious decision to sin*. Any sin will separate us from God. God will not justify sin to be acceptable. Man may rationalize this action to be acceptable, but God does not.

Homosexuality has terrible results for the people who partake of this sin. God says homosexuality is an abomination. It's wrong according to God's word. Satan will convince a person that sin is right. Sin is never right; it is always wrong.

> If a man lies with a male as he lies with a woman,
> both of them have committed an abomination.
> They shall be put to death. Their blood shall be
> upon them. (Lev. 20:13 NKJV)

Men and women are dishonoring their bodies by living the homosexual lifestyle. Their disgraceful desires betray their hearts into living a lie. They serve their sinful passions and the creature within, rather than the Creator. They forsake all natural relations for unnatural ones. Not only that, but they are committing indecent acts: men with men; women with women.

> Therefore God also gave them up to uncleanness,
> in lust of their hearts, to dishonor their bodies
> among themselves, who exchange the truth of
> God for the lie, and worshiped and served the
> creature rather than the creator, who is blessed

> forever. Amen! For this reason God gave them up to vile passions. For even their women exchanged the natural use for what is against nature. Likewise also the men, leaving the natural use of the woman, burned in their lust for one another, men with men committing what is shameful, and receiving in themselves the penalty of their error which was due. (Rom. 1:24–27 NKJV)

Vile: it is morally despicable, repulsive, disgusting, contemptible.

Sin has a way of clouding our judgment. Satan is the master of deception, deceit, and false hope. Occasionally, it's hard for us to see what the truth is and what the lie is. God does not want us to be deceived into believing a lie. Satan can paint a picture that sin is acceptable if we rationalize our action of sin to be right. Paul wrote the Corinthians not to keep company with sexually immoral people. Reference to 1 Corinthians 5:9.

People who live this lifestyle of homosexuality will not inherit the kingdom of God. They are looked at by God as detestable and having committed an act of abomination to the Lord.

Detestable: intense dislike
Abomination: extreme disgust, hatred

The unrighteous will not inherit the kingdom of God.

> Do you not know that the unrighteous will not inherit the kingdom of God? Do not be deceived. Neither fornicators, nor idolaters, nor adulterers, nor homosexuals, nor sodomites, nor thieves, nor covetous, nor drunkards, nor revilers, nor extortioners will inherit the kingdom of God. (1 Cor. 6:9–10 NKJV)

SEXUAL IMMORALITY

Fornicator: consensual sexual intercourse between two persons not married to each other. This is an act of sexual immorality.

Idolater: a person who is a worshiper of idols

Adulterer: a person who voluntarily has sexual intercourse, between a married man and someone besides his wife, or between a married woman and someone besides her husband. This is an act of sexual immorality.

Homosexual: is a person who has a sexual desire toward another of the same sex Homosexual is a person who has sexual relations with a person of the same sex. This is an act of sexual immorality.

Sodomite: is a person who has anal or oral sexual intercourse with a member of the same or opposite sex, also sexual intercourse with an animal. This is an act of sexual immorality.

Thief: is a person that steals secretly, also one who commits larceny

Covetous: a person who has a desire for wealth, or possessions, or for another's possessions, a lack of restraint, and often of discrimination in desire to have status symbols. An implication of selfishness and often suggests unfair or ruthlessness.

Drunkard: a person impaired by alcohol, a level of alcohol in the blood that exceeds a maximum prescribed by law, legally drunk, being intoxicated

Reviler: is a verbally abusive person

Extortioner: is a person who obtains something by force, intimidation, or undue illegal power from a person

People say they have rights, and God will have to accept them as they are, or He is not a God of love. God is love. He is just. He is the creator of the universe. We are the creation, not the creator. What God thinks is what is important. What God calls sin is sin! We cannot rationalize our action of sin to be right.

The law is not made for the righteous but for the: lawless and insubordinate, ungodly and sinners, unholy and profane, murders of fathers and mothers, man-slayers, fornicators, sodomites, kidnappers, liars, perjurers, and anything that is country to sound doctrine. Reference to 1 Timothy 1:8–10.

It is sin to engage in sexual activity outside the institute of marriage, one man and one woman. This is the way God outlined it in Scripture. Many people try to convince themselves that the sin of sexual immorality is there right. Some people say they have been born with this as their makeup as a person. God intended for man to be with woman in marriage. Man is with woman, and woman is with man, or they stay apart!

Many people who claim to be homosexual claim it is their right. Sin is not a right. Sin is disobedience to God. Homosexuality does not differ from adultery where a person makes *a conscious decision* to act a certain way. People rationalize their decision of a sexual immoral lifestyle as being an acceptable way of life, and God will just have to accept it. It just does not work that way. As Christians, *we are to love the person, not the sin.*

Lust wants something so bad that you set common sense aside. Passion becomes a driving force that overrules good, sound thinking in a sexual context. Lust can be the desire for illicit sex. Illicit would be anything that is not permitted, unlawful, and what God has said not to do. The Scripture makes us aware and tells us that lust leads to sin. If you choose this behavior, *you are making a conscious decision to sin.* Our passion for lust, when not controlled, will lead to immoral sex. When you lust for sex outside of marriage, it leads to sin. God did not intend sex outside of marriage for man or woman. Sex outside of marriage is man's ability to perverse what God made for good. In marriage between a man and a woman, passion will fuel the desire for your mate, the one you choose to spend the rest of your life with.

> But I say to you that whoever looks at a woman
> to lust for her has already committed adultery
> with her in his heart. (Matt. 5:28 NKJV)

God looks at our hearts. The heart shows our true desire, what we believe. Our outward appearance can mask our desires. The heart reveals who we are and defines what we are. A man looking at a woman, or a woman looking at a man, with thoughts of wanting that person the same way a person wants their wife or husband is a sin. Guard your heart and train your mind to think of the things of God. It can be done.

We should endeavor to live a lifestyle that works to make us better. A life that shows the good in us instead of the selfishness.

> Let us walk properly, as in the day, not in revelry and drunkenness, not in lewdness and lust, not in strife and envy. (Rom. 13:13 NKJV)

Selfishness is a part of our sinful nature. Each one of us are born with and has to deal with every day.

> But each one is tempted when he is drawn away by his own desires and enticed. Then, when desire has conceived, it gives birth to sin, and sin, when it is full-grown, brings forth death. (James 1:14–15 NKJV)

Sin, in any form, will bring death. Separation from God is the result of sin. When sin entices and tempts us, it always looks desirable at the beginning. People have a hard time telling what the lie is. Satan has convinced people that the lie is the truth for centuries. The desire of man, if not focused on God, will lead to sin, which leads to death. "They will give account to Him who is ready to judge the living and the dead" (1 Pet. 4:5 NKJV).

We need to learn from the dark in the past and stay in the light. God in all His glory is light, and Satan in all of his evil is darkness. When evil steps into the light, it becomes uneasy. The lies show they are false. Satan will pull blinders over our eyes a little at a time if we don't remain focused on God, and we will lose track of what is good. The sad thing is we let him do it to us.

Incest is sex with a close relative other than one's spouse. Scripture prohibits this action. The King James Version uses the term "to uncover the nakedness," which means to sleep with as husband

and wife. If you choose this behavior, *you are making a conscious decision to sin.*

Do not have sex with a close relative. Define a close relative, fathers—your mother, your father's wife—not your mother—your sister, your father's daughter, or your mother's daughter. It does not matter if she is born in your house or somewhere else. Do not have sexual encounters with your son's daughter or your daughter's daughter. You are not to have sex with your father's sister or your mother's sister. Do not have sex with your brother's wife. She is your aunt. Never have sex with a woman and her daughter. Don't have sex with either her son's daughter or her daughter's daughter. Do not have sex with your wife's sister. These are close relatives, and that would be wickedness. Reference to Leviticus 18:6–18.

As we review the list of brothers, sisters, aunts, uncles and see how the list grows, we wonder why it goes into such depth. Wouldn't it be easier to just say, don't have sexual relations with a close relative? The writers must have known what the lawyers would have done, find a loophole to create an exception. The first basic rule to remember is how God looks at sin, any kind of sin, as disobedience. This disobedience to Him brings separation. The second basic rule is to remember that God knows everything.

This relationship, this bond between a married man and a woman, is of great importance. The husband and wife are so important to the success and establishment of the family. When we go outside of what God set up for marriage, it destroys the family. If we live in sin, there is only one thing that can happen. It will separate us from God.

All these—adultery, bestiality, homosexuality, lust, incest—are sexual immorality. It is sin, and it destroys our relationship with God.

Good sex, sex within marriage, one man and one woman, is a gift from God and is to be enjoyed and celebrated by both husband and wife. Sex is a natural blessing between husband and wife, one man and one woman. The two become one. This gives great joy and satisfaction to both parties and strengthens the two toward each other to become one.

SEXUAL IMMORALITY

> Drink from your own well, my son-be faithful and true to your wife. Why should you beget children with women of the street? Why share your children with those outside your home? Let your manhood be a blessing; rejoice in the wife of your youth. Let her charms and tender embrace satisfy you. Let her love alone fill you with delight. Why delight yourself with prostitutes, embracing what isn't yours? For God is closely watching you, and he weights carefully everything you do. (Prov. 5:15–21 LB)

Be true to the love of your youth. Don't let sin come into your life and destroy your family. Trust is a bond that can stand against all odds. When you violate this trust by sexual misconduct, it will be very hard, if not impossible, to reacquire the trust. You can restore a trust, but this new trust is never quite the same. We weaken the unity by the trust that was abused. The trust that stands against sexual immorality will be strong and will grow. The couple will cherish this trust into their golden years.

> Marriage should be honored by all, and the marriage bed kept pure, for God will judge the adulterer and all the sexually immoral. (Heb. 13:4 NIV)

Men and women will do many splendid things in their lifetime. One thing that every person has to protect is his or her faithfulness to their spouse. This bond, this love, and nurturing is one of God's gifts to men and women. This bond helps us live a full and purposeful life. God has given each of us so many gifts, and this is one of the more special gifts that the Lord has bestowed on us. The gift of trust, faithfulness ties us together and keeps us strong in the face of adversity and sexual temptations.

Christians can stay pure by living according to God's word. "How can a young man keep his way pure? By living according to your word" (Ps. 119:9 NIV). Learn God's word and keep it in your heart. "Your word I have hidden in my heart, that I might not sin against You" (Ps. 119:11 NKJV).

We must *make a conscious decision* to live according to God's word. "I have made a covenant with my eyes; Why then should I look upon a young woman?" (Job 31:1 NKJV).

Our eyes are what we see with and where temptation begins. We walk under the leadership of the Holy Spirit. Sanctification is through the Spirit, not the law. We are set apart to be pure of heart, honest and trustworthy, and living to be more like Jesus. Being a Christian is a daily affair. Not just on Sunday morning and evening and Wednesday evening when the church assembles to worship our Lord, we are to be Christian each day, each hour, and each minute.

> So I say, live by the Spirit, and you will not gratify the desires of sinful nature. For the sinful nature desires what is contrary to the Spirit, and the Spirit what is contrary to the sinful nature. They are in conflict with each other, so that you do not do what you want. But if you are led by the Spirit, you are not under the law. (Gal. 5:16–18 NIV)

The acts of sinful nature are obvious:
Sexual immorality, impurity, debauchery, idolatry, witchcraft, hatred, discord, fits of rage, self-ambition, dissension, faction and envy, drunkenness, orgies and the like.

He warns us that those who live like this will not inherit the kingdom of God. Reference to Galatians 5:19–21.

Sexual immorality: Adultery, bestiality, homosexuality, lust, incest, pornography, fornication, an immoral act, any practice involving sex outside of marriage. Acceptable marriage is between one man and one woman.
Impurity: something unclean, mixed with something unwanted, thought, act, or substance

SEXUAL IMMORALITY

Debauchery: indulgence in immoral bodily pleasures, especially sexual pleasures
Idolatry: worship of a physical object as god
Witchcraft: using sorcery or magic and in communication with the devil
Hatred: extreme dislike or disgust
Discord: lack of agreement or harmony, quarreling, conflict
Jealousy: an attitude or feeling, covetousness, envy, resentment
Fits of rage: actions of violent wrath and uncontrolled anger
Self-ambition: a desire for fame or power
Dissension: partisan, contentiously quarreling, strife
Factions of envy: a resentful awareness, malice
Drunkenness: excessive use of alcohol, intoxication
Orgies: a sexual encounter involving many people with excessive indulgence, with a sexual appetite or craving

The Spirit gives victory over sin. Christian character is not by self-effort. The Holy Spirit produces Christian character. Flee, run from sexual temptation, and pursue righteousness. Faith, love, peace, call on the Lord out of a pure heart. Reference to 2 Timothy 2:22.

God dealt with the people in the Old Testament when they had a total disregard for His commandments. The people who lived in Sodom and Gomorrah immersed their lives in sexual depravity, adultery, bestiality, homosexuality, and incest. They were living in sexual bondage with no regard for God's law. This society partook of some of the most perverse acts known to man. They knew no bounds in their lust for sexual pleasure and self-gratification. They reached a new low for man. They found the most horrible way to go astray from God. Their lust for themselves and the pleasure that it brought them was their undoing. God could not let this gross abuse of sin go on any farther than it went. He destroyed them in an extremely violent and destructive manner. The Lord sent fire and brimstone down on all that lived in Sodom and Gomorrah. There was no question in anyone's mind that God would not permit this behavior. People just never seem to learn that God's truth doesn't change, and it's forever. It does not matter how we rationalize the sin in our life, sin is sin in

God's eyes, no exceptions, *period*! God cannot, and will not, rationalize sin to be okay. The more we separate ourselves from God's principles and love, the more we put our self-interest above others and the farther we move away from God.

They formed this great nation of ours on the right to have religious freedom, freedom from religious persecution. The more laws we make reinforcing the rights of individuals over right and wrong, the farther we move away from God. The belief in God was the foundation that was the guiding light of our Founding Fathers. Our nation is on a collision course with destruction. When people flaunt their sin in front of God for all to see and say, "It is my right," and the majority does not stop it, we are going down the wrong path. There is a difference between individual rights and right and wrong. Sin and perversion boast of individual rights. They hinder and stop what is right. Satan deceives us into believing that our rights are more important than doing what is right. By doing something that is wrong because it is our right, we convince ourselves it's okay, then we have deceived ourselves.

Sex is such a powerful force in our lives and can control us in ways that we lose our self-control. We need to stay focused on God. Sex drive can destroy us and ones around us. It becomes an addiction, and thus we start to abuse it. When we abuse it, it becomes perverse. Sex is the most beautiful thing that God gave to man and woman in marriage. When done God's way, man and woman become one, and this is the unseen force that strengthens the two. Sex between a man and a woman is the only acceptable form that God will acknowledge and bless. Sex only becomes evil outside of marriage.

CHAPTER 8

The Seventy Weeks of Daniel

A FEW QUESTIONS NEED TO be looked at when discussing the Seventy Weeks of Daniel. Why does Daniel use the term *week* instead of *years*? What is the significance of sixty-two weeks, seven weeks, and one week, which comprise the Seventy Weeks of Daniel? If there is no significance between sixty-two weeks and seven weeks, why didn't he just use the term sixty-nine weeks? Why does Daniel use the term *weeks* in this section of chapter 9 instead of *years* as he has done in chapters 7, 8, 9, 10? If Daniel changed the term from *years* to *weeks*, why does everyone want to change it back to years? Is Daniel talking about his past, present, and future? If Daniel is talking about his future, how far in the future is he talking about? Is Daniel talking about his past, his future, or is he talking about our past his future, or is he talking about our past and our future? Can the Seventy Weeks refer to a prophecy of his time and contain a prophecy of our future at the same time? Could it have a dual meaning?

The prophecy of the Seventy Weeks of Daniel has three distinct divisions; and they are sixty-two weeks, seven weeks, and one week. The sixty-two weeks leads up to the cross, the seven weeks start after the cross, the one week is in two halves, and the cross is in the middle. The church age, the seven weeks, is here to reach the lost. God's love is for all to come to know Him. Jesus will not return until every person has heard the word of God, the plan of salvation. Christ died and rose so all (Jew and Gentile) could come to know Him. The final week, the cross, is in the middle. At the end of the sixty-two weeks and start of the seven weeks is the cross. The cross is in the middle of the final week. First half of the final week is Christ's life and the cross. Second half of the final week is at the end of the seven weeks. The first half of the final week talks about peace, and the second half of the final week talks about great pain and suffering. This will be the worst persecution the world has ever seen.

Daniel uses years at the start of each of these chapters.

Chapter 7: "In the first year of Belshazzar King of Babylon…"

Chapter 8: "In the third year of the reign of King Belshazzar…"

Chapter 9: "In the first year of Darius…"

Chapter 10: "In the third year of Cyrus King of Persia…" This places Daniel in history.

Chapter 9 starts with years, then in verse 20, it changes to weeks. Daniel uses the term weeks in chapter 9 verses 24–27 and in chapter 10 verses 2–3. The weeks in chapter 9 are referring to segments of time. They consider world history before the second coming of Christ. What is the root number of seventy and three? They are seven and three. The weeks refer to the number seven, which means completeness, to bring an end to human history. The three refers to the three sections of the seventy weeks of Daniel; and they are six-two weeks, seven weeks, and one week. Seven and three are powerful numbers in the Bible. When they are used, we should pay attention. There is great meaning being revealed to us.

Chapters 7, 8, and 9 of Daniel is talking about things that are happening around Daniel's time and in his future and about things yet to come in our future. It talks about kings and empires that you can see in history. In chapter 7 of Daniel, it talks about the four beast: the first world empire (Babylon), the second world empire (Mido-Persia), the third world empire (Greece), the fourth world empire (Rome). Revelation chapter 13 talks about the beast of the sea and the beast of the earth. In the end times, the seven heads could be Egypt, Assyria, Babylon, Greece, Persia, Rome, and a restored Roman Empire. The ten horns could be the final form of the Gentile world power. The beast symbolizes both a revived Roman Empire and a specific ruler, the Antichrist.

Many have looked at the prophecy referred to in Daniel one way, then another. When Christ returns, that is when we will know and understand. Anytime you are looking at prophecy, you need to bathe it in prayer.

The one thing we can all agree on is we are to be about our Father's business. We are to be telling a lost world about the Savior, Jesus Christ, until He returns. We are to tell the people we encounter what we know and have experienced, not what the other guy has experienced but what we have experienced.

The seventy weeks of Danie's prophecy, found in Daniel 9:20–27, are separated into seven sections:

1. Daniel 9:20–23 NKJV

   Now while I was speaking, praying, and confessing my sin and the sin of my people Israel, and presenting my supplication before the Lord my God for the holy mountain of my God, yes, while I was speaking in prayer, the man Gabriel, whom I had seen in the vision at the beginning, being caused to fly swiftly, reached me about the time of the evening offering. And he informed me, and talked with me, and said, "O Daniel, I have now come forth to give you skill to understand. At the beginning of your supplications the command went out, and I have come to tell you, for you are greatly beloved; therefore consider the matter, and understand vision."

2. Daniel 9:24 NKJV

   Seventy weeks are determined for your people and for your holy city, to finish the transgression, to make an end of sins, to make reconciliation for iniquity, to bring in everlasting righteousness, to seal up vision and prophecy, and to anoint the Most Holy.

3. Daniel 9:25 NKJV

Know therefore and understand, that from the going forth of the command, to restore and rebuild Jerusalem, until Messiah the Prince, there shall be seven weeks and sixty-two weeks; the street shall be built again, and the wall, even in troublesome times.

4. Daniel 9:26a NKJV

And after the sixty-two weeks, Messiah shall be cut off, but not for Himself.

5. Daniel 9:26b NKJV

And the people of the prince who is to come, shall destroy the city and the sanctuary. The end of it shall be with a flood, and till the end of the war desolations are determined.

6. Daniel 9:27a NKJV

Then he shall confirm a covenant with many for one week; but in the middle of the week he shall bring an end to sacrifice and offering.

7. Daniel 9:27b NKJV

And on the wing of abomination shall be one who makes desolate, even until the consummation, which is determined, is poured out on the desolate.

People have been saying that the weeks talked about in Daniel 9 should be years. What if the weeks talked about in Daniel 9 are segments of time. He chose the weeks because it represents the number seven, which means complete. The New King James Version, in verse 24, starts off with "Seventy weeks are determined." In the New International Version, it says, "Seventy, 'sevens' are decreed" Some say weeks don't show a specific number of years but a period of time. God, in His mercy, can do whatever He wants. There are many accounts and interpretations of world history before Christ's second coming. The sevens in these verses represent the completion of human history.

Daniel was praying—confessing his sins and the sins of his people, presenting his request humbly, and expressing in reverence to the Lord. He was speaking in prayer, and the man, Gabriel, whom he had seen in a vision earlier, was flying swiftly and came to him at the evening offering. He talked with Daniel and told him, "O Daniel, I have now come forth to give you skill to understand. I tell you; you are loved; therefore, consider the matter and understand the vision." Reference to Daniel 9:20–23.

Daniel was praying, confessing the sins of his people. Daniel says, "Yes, while I was speaking in prayer, the man Gabriel..." Gabriel came to him and said, "I have come to give you understanding. You are greatly beloved; consider the matter, and understand the vision." It's interesting that Daniel uses the term "the man Gabriel." Do humans resemble angels? Gabriel is still angelic. Genesis talks about who man is like.

Then God said, "Let Us make man in Our image, according to Our likeness" (Gen. 1:26a NKJV).

Where it says, "Make man in Our image... Our likeness." *Our* is capitalized because it is talking about the Trinity: God the Father, God the Son, and God the Holy Spirit.

The Temple was in ruins, so daily sacrifices were hard, if not impossible. Daniel used this time for his worship and prayers. Daniel's prayer was his evening offering. For an angel, a messenger of God, to say, "You are greatly beloved," was a blessing. This had to encourage and please Daniel.

> Seventy weeks are determined for your people and for your holy city, to finish the transgression, to make an end of sins, to make reconciliation for iniquity, to bring in everlasting righteousness, to seal up vision and prophecy, and to anoint the Most Holy. (Dan. 9:24 NKJV)

Christ will return for His church, His believers. It talks about the completeness of time, that man has to correct his sins and change his ways. God created and loves all of us. God chose the nation of Israel to be His chosen people. He desires fellowship with all of us. When talking about Daniel's vision, we need to determine if the vision refers to precross, God's choose people Israel, or postcross, Christ's church. From Daniel's time, the future can mean either pre-cross or postcross.

The prophecy talks about all people, not just the Jews, to make an end to sin. Christ died on the cross for all our sins, then in three days He rose victorious. This is for every man, woman, and child. It does not matter from what walk of life you come from. Christ is the cornerstone of this whole prophecy. Everything hinges on the cross. If you look at all six points in verse 24, it incorporates the cross and His return.

> Know therefore and understand, that from the going forth of the command, to restore and rebuild Jerusalem, until Messiah the Prince, there shall be seven weeks and sixty-two weeks; the street shall be built again, and the wall, even in troublesome times. (Dan. 9:25 NKJV)

The command is that within seven weeks and sixty-two weeks, the holy city Jerusalem, the walls and the streets, is to be rebuilt before Christ's returns. It doesn't matter what is going on, it must be accomplished in good times and bad times, "even in time of trouble." They have both the sixty-two weeks and seven weeks to rebuild the streets and the wall of Jerusalem.

THE SEVENTY WEEKS OF DANIEL

Some people think that the sixty-two weeks and the seven weeks go together to get to the cross. Something happened at the end of the sixty-two weeks. These two are together to rebuild the streets and the wall before Christ's return, not the cross. The cross is at the end of one of these, not both of them. The cross is at the end of the sixty-two weeks and the beginning of the seven weeks.

> And after the sixty-two weeks, messiah shall be cut off, but not for Himself. (Dan. 9:26a NKJV)

There is no mention of the seven weeks in verse 26. The cross is at the end of the sixty-two weeks. The cross is at the beginning of the seven weeks. "Messiah shall be cut off," this is a reference to the crucifixion of Jesus Christ. Christ died on the cross for the sins of the world, not for His sins. He had no sin.

> And the people of the prince who is to come, shall destroy the city and the sanctuary. The end of it shall be with a flood, and till the end of the war desolations are determined. (Dan. 9:26b NKJV)

"And the people of the prince who is to come," this is reference to the Antichrist, "shall destroy the city and the sanctuary." The Antichrist will destroy. And "the end will be with a flood," in the book of Revelation, chapter 12, the woman of Israel, and the birth of a male child. The dragon, Satan, is there waiting to devour the child; but the child is caught up to be with God. The woman flees to the wilderness to a place God has prepared for her. Michael and his angels fought with the dragon and cast him down to earth. This enrages the dragon, and the dragon set out to persecute the woman who gave birth to the child. She has wings to fly into the wilderness to be nourished. The serpent spewed water from his mouth like a flood, after the woman. The earth helped the woman by opening and swallowing up the flood. "And until the end of the war of desolation, are determined." The seven seals, the seven trumpets, and the seven bowls are the three sevens. They are warnings and judgments and wrath. God judges Babylon, and then the battle of Armageddon will come at God's appointed time.

"Then he shall confirm a covenant with many for one week; but in the middle of the week he shall bring an end to sacrifice and offering" (Dan. 9:27a NKJV). He shall confirm a new covenant. Jesus is the new covenant of grace, not the law. Gentiles are the many, the poor, and the common people. The New Testament is about the church. The first half of the final week is when Jesus walked among us on earth. Jesus brought peace, an eternal peace, from God. This peace, no one can take from you. No matter what is going on around you. A peace that comes from God will see you through whatever is happening. "But in the middle of the week he shall bring an end to sacrifice and offering." The crucifixion of Jesus Christ became the only sacrifice we need. Jew or Gentile, Jesus is the only way to the Father. We only need to ask to be a child of God, and He will make us complete. Jesus became the only sacrifice that God will accept.

"And on the wing of abomination shall be one who makes desolate, even until the consummation, which is determined, is poured out on the desolate" (Dan. 9:27b NKJV). "And on the wings of abominations shall be one who makes desolate." In Matthew, it talks about the abomination and desolation in the middle of the week. The cross is in the middle of the final week.

"Therefore when you see the abomination of the desolation, spoken of by Daniel the prophet, standing in the holy place." (Whoever reads, let him understand.)

> Then let those who are in Judea flee to the mountains. Let him who is on the housetop not go down to take anything out of his house. And let him who is in the field not go back to get his clothes. But woe to those who are pregnant and to those who are nursing babies in those days! And pray that your flight may not be in winter or on the Sabbath. (Matt. 24:15–20 NKJV)

There will be one whom Christians will loath and have extreme disgust for. Even until the consummation, which is to be determined, this hardship will continue until the end when Christ returns.

In Romans, it talks about the blindness that happened to Israel. This will continue until the fullness of the Gentiles come. Then Israel's eyes will be opened, and they will be able to see and understand who Christ is, our Savior, the Messiah. Christ's name means Messiah.

> What then? Israel has not obtained what it seeks; but the elect have obtained it, and the rest were blinded. Just as it is written God has given them a spirit of stupor, Eyes that they should not see, And ears that they should not hear, to this very day. (Rom. 11:7–8 NKJV)

> For I do not desire, brethren, that you should be ignorant of this mystery, lest you should be wise in your own opinion, that blindness in part has happened to Israel until the fullness of the Gentiles has come in. (Rom. 11:25 NKJV)

The sixty-two weeks were before the cross, the seven weeks were after the cross, and the cross was in the middle of the final week. In the final week, the first half is at the end of the sixty-two weeks and ends with the cross, and the second half of the final weeks at the end of the seven weeks. The sixty-two weeks ends with the cross, the seven weeks begin with the cross, and finish with the return of Christ. The final week starts with Christ's ministry on earth and ends with the Antichrist's reign on earth. The concluding half of the final week ends with Christ's return. Christ was approximately thirty-five and a half years old at the cross (Christ was born in 4 BC and was crucified in AD 30). His ministry was three and a half years long, and the cross was in the middle of the final week.

There are two possibilities for the sixty-two weeks, the seven weeks, and the final week. The first possibility would use the sixty-two weeks, the seven weeks, and the final week as a total picture of humanity from start to finish, from Adam to Christ's return. The second possibility would use the sixty-two weeks, the seven weeks, and the final week to be a picture of the start of His chosen people to the finish, from Abraham to Christ's return. It could be both. God may have given us a glimpse of His glory, making both of these be what He has accomplished and going to accomplish.

What is in a name in the Old Testament time? How much stock did they put in their names? Your name meant something to God. You're worthy. If God changed your name, it was a noteworthy event. A name change: the old ended and the new began.

The First Possibility for Sixty-Two Weeks

Genesis 5:1–32 lists the descendants of Adam: Adam to Shem.
Genesis 11:10–26 lists the descendants of Shem: Shem to Abraham.
Matthew 1:1–16 lists the genealogy of Jesus: Abraham to Jesus.
There are sixty generations from Adam to Christ using the legal lineage of Joseph to Christ:
Generations from Adam to Noah (Gen. 5:1–32):
Reference to 1 Chronicles 1:1–14

- Adam, Seth, Enosh, Cainan, Mahalalel, Jared, Enoch, Methsuelah, Lamech, Noah

Generations from Shem to Abraham (Gen. 11:10–26):
Reference to 1 Chronicles 1:17–27

- Shem, Arphaxad, Salah (Shelah), Eber, Peleg, Reu, Serug, Nahor, Terah, Abram

God changed Abram's name to Abraham (Gen. 17:15).
Generations from Isaac to David (Matt. 1:1–6a):
Reference to Ruth 4:18-22, 1 Chronicles 2:1–5

- Abraham, Isaac, Jacob, Judah, Perez, Hezron, Ram, Amminadah, Nahshon, Salmon, Boaz, Obed, Jesse, David

God changed the name of Jacob to Israel (Gen. 32:28).

In Matthew, it uses the legal lineage from David, to Joseph, to Christ. In Luke, it takes the path of physical lineage from David, to Mary, to Christ. Christ was born to a virgin, Mary. You can trace lineages, legal through Joseph and physical through Mary, from David to Jesus. It does not matter which person you want to use, Joseph or Mary, both can be traced to David. And David can be traced to Abraham, and Abraham to Noah, and Noah to Adam.

Generations from David to Joseph to Jesus Christ (Matt. 1:6b–11):

- *David*, Solomon, Rehoboam, Abijah, Ash, Jehoshaphat, Joram, Uzziah, Jotham, Ahaz, Hezekiah, Manasseh, Amon, Josiah, Jeconiah, Shealtie, Zerubbabel, Adiud, Eliakim, Azor, Zadok, Achim, Eliud, Eleazar, Matthan, Jacob, Joseph, *Jesus Christ*

Generation from David to Mary to Jesus Christ (Luke 3:23–31):

- *David*, Nathan, Mattathah, Menan, Melea, Eliakim, Jonan, Joseph, Judah, Simeon, Levi, Matthat, Jorim, Eliezer, Jose, Er, Elmodam, Cosam, Addi, Melchi, Neri, Shealtier, Zerubbabel, Rhesa, Joannas, Judah, Joseph, Semei, Mattathiah, Maath, Naggai, Esli, Nahum, Amos, Mattathiah, Joseph, Janna, Melchi, Levi, Mastthat, Heli, Mary, *Jesus Christ*

God changed the names of two men who showed great faith in God. Abram's name changed to Abraham, and Jacob's name changed to Israel. Abraham was the father of God's chosen people. Jacob's children became the twelve tribes of Israel. Each man and each name and changed name is noteworthy. There are sixty generations from Adam to Jesus. The names God changed—Abram to Abraham and Jacob to Israel—are changes that God did, and that makes sixty-two.

IS THERE TIME

The Second Possibility for Sixty-Two Weeks

For people who like to crunch the numbers. Abraham was born in 2176 BC. The time of the Jews is Abraham to the crucifixion of Christ. The crucifixion was in AD 30. The birth of Abraham to Christ's death on the cross is 2,207 years (2176 + 30 + 1 = 2207). If you divide 2207 by 62, you get 35.5. The time Jesus lived and walked on this earth is estimated at 35.5 years, birth *four years* before BC + *one year* for zero + *thirty years* AD + *half year*, 4 + 1 + 30 + 1/2 = 35.5 years. It is interesting that there were sixty-two of Christ's life span from Abraham's birth to Christ's death on the cross. Maybe the sixty-two is a picture of humanity, Adam to Christ, or maybe it is a picture of God's chosen people, Abraham to Christ. Maybe it's both.

> And after the sixty-two weeks Messiah shall be cut off, but not for Himself… (Dan. 9:26a NKJV)

Sixty-two weeks ends with the cross. This is the time of the Jews, the time leading up to the cross. Seven weeks start with the cross. The church age is the time of the Gentiles. First half of the final week comes at the end of the sixty-two weeks. Second half of the final week comes at the end of the seven weeks, the church age. In the middle of end-time tribulation is the cross. It separates the time of the Jews from the time of the Gentiles. The time of the Jews is up to the cross and the time of the Gentile is form the cross to the return of Christ. The second half of the final week is in the great tribulation and the end of the church age. You have God's chosen people, the Jews, and Christ's church. We who believe and accepted Christ as our personal Savior, all are a part of the family of God because He adopted the church into His family. Peace and providing a way back to God is in the final week. The transition from the End-Time Tribulation to the Great Tribulation is between the seals and the trumpets. The Great Tribulation will be so very harsh. Even during this persecution that will be going on, God has a way back to Him in place.

THE SEVENTY WEEKS OF DANIEL

The first half of the final week is peace, and Jesus is that peace. It is an inner peace that no one can take from us. Jesus brought peace that will endure, even during any kind of tribulation. God provided a way back to a right relationship with Him. Jesus brought hope in a time when persecution was at an all-time high. People had devised new ways to hurt and inflict pain on itself. Humanity would rather live in sin instead of worshipping the creator of the universe. There is a gap in the middle of the final week, and that is the church age. The church age is the seven weeks.

The concluding half of the final week is the worst persecution the world has ever seen or will ever see. In the final half of the final week is the Great Tribulation. God gives humanity a final chance to repent. God has given us signs of His coming judgments. He will warn everyone. He will announce His judgments are here and ready to be dispensed to the earth and man. Seals are the warnings to let everyone know the Great Tribulation is ready to start. The Great Tribulation will start with the trumpets. God's judgment will come after the seals warning. Satan is cast out of heaven down to earth. Satan has authority for forty-two months to overcome all who dwell on the earth. It's interesting to note that Jesus's ministry was forty-two months and Satan's authority after being cast down to earth is forty-two months.

In the trumpets and the bowls, God will judge the earth and man. Then God will judge the harlot, Babylon. The trumpets in John's day were the sound that war was beginning. God will be making war on evil.

The first half of the final week, is about providing a way for sinful man to return to fellowship and worship a loving God. The second half of the final week is about judgments.

The seals are about warning signs that tell us to repent. It tells us judgment is here, and then judgment begins upon the earth and man.

Christ was born in 4 BC. Jesus's death took place during the spring of AD 30. Jesus was thirty-five when He went to the cross and died for our sins, which amounts to five sevens. Remember, seven is the number of completeness. It's not a coincidence that Jesus would relate to the number seven.

In the seals, the term *great* is used only once, the sixth seal (6:12), great earthquake. The great tribulation will be a part of the last part of the final week. Starting with the end of the seals, the term *great* starts to appear in the book of Revelation. In the New King James version: 8:8, great mountain burning; 8:10, great star fell from heaven; 11:19, great hail; 12:9, great dragon; 12:12, great wrath; and 16:18, great earthquake.

$$62 \text{ weeks} + 7 \text{ weeks} + 1 \text{ week} = 70 \text{ weeks}$$
62 weeks: the cross is at the end of the sixty-two weeks
7 weeks: the cross is at the start of the seven weeks
1 week: the cross is in the middle of the final week

There are signs in Revelation when the seals, trumpets, and bowls have finished before the next one is about to start:

End of the Seals (Rev. 8:5 NKJV)	There were noises, thunderings, lightnings, and an earthquake.
End of the Trumpets (Rev. 11:19 NKJV)	There were lightnings, noises, thunderings, an earthquake, and great hail.
End of the Bowls (Rev.16:18 NKJV)	And there were noises and thunderings and lightnings: there was a great earthquake as had not occurred since men were on the earth.

Christians, the church will go through the great tribulation. The Laodicean church age is lukewarm. It is the church of indifference, the last of the church age. This is at the end of the Great Tribulation.

THE SEVENTY WEEKS OF DANIEL

The Final Week

The First Half		The Second Half
1. Announcement of Jesus birth to Mary and Joseph. God tells of His Son to come to save the world.	C	1. The seals, warnings God warns the time has arrived to repent.
2. The birth of Jesus Arrival of the Son of God	R	2. The trumpets, judgment God announces judgment is coming. Repent, the great tribulation is starting.
3. Jesus ministry for forty-two months Christ lives and explains God's plan, salvation		3. Satan is cast out of heaven and rules for forty-two months. Authority given him over every tribe, tongue, and nation.
4. Jesus's ministry Men are astounded at Christ's knowledge	O	4. The bowls God wrath.
5. Jesus accused of sin and He had no sin. The Jews abandoned the Savior.		5. A woman and the beast God deals with the harlot, Babylon.
6. Jesus Death and burial	S	6. Satan Defeated, judged, and sentenced, the eternal lake of fire.
7. Christ Christ's Resurrection The end of the first half of the final week.	S	7. Christ Chris's return, victory is Christ's The end of the second half of the final week.

IS THERE TIME

Satan has authority to make war on the saints for forty-two months, that's three and a half years. Three and a half years is the same time as Christ's ministry here on earth. Interesting.

> And he was given a mouth speaking great things and blasphemy, and he was given authority to continue for forty-two months. (Rev. 13:5 NKJV)

> It was granted to him to make war with the saints and to overcome them. And authority was given him over every tribe, tongue, and nation. All who dwell on the earth will worship him, whose names have not been written in the Book of Life of the Lamb slain from the foundation of the world. If anyone has an ear, let him hear. (Rev. 13:7–9 NKJV)

There will be a remnant of Christians, the church, the saints until the end when Christ returns. Anyone saved after the cross and until the return of Christ is adopted into the family of God.

Joseph married Mary, the mother of Jesus, and had no relations as husband and wife until after the birth of Jesus. Jesus was born of a virgin.

> Now the birth of Jesus Christ was as follows: After His mother Mary was betrothed to Joseph, before they came together, she was found with child of the Holy Spirit. (Matt. 1:18 NKJV)

Joseph, not wanting to make a public example of Mary, he thought about putting her away secretly.

> But while he thought about these things, behold, an angel of the Lord appeared to him in a dream, saying, "Joseph, son of David, do not be afraid to take to you Mary your wife, for that which is

conceived in her is of the Holy Spirit." (Matt. 1:20 NKJV)

The prophet Isaiah, many years earlier, prophesied about the virgin birth of Jesus; and Matthew quoted him here:

> Therefore the Lord Himself will give you a sign: Behold, the virgin shall conceive and bear a Son, and shall call His name Immanuel. (Isa. 7:14 NKJV)

> Behold, the virgin shall be with child, and bear a Son, and they shall call His name Immanuel, which is translated, God with us. (Matt. 1:23 NKJV)

At the end of the sixty-two weeks is the cross. The cross is at the start of the seven weeks, and the cross is in the middle of the final week. The cross is what ties this prophecy together. All three hinge on the cross.

CHAPTER 9

Church Age

THE CHURCH AGE STARTED WITH the cross. The world under the Roman Empire was a time when a king or an emperor had control over people's lives, literally life and death. Horrible things could happen to people in bondage. People in those days who had servants didn't look at other people as being one of God's creations. Rather, as property and the owner, they could do pretty much whatever they wanted with them.

The thought process was, if you were a person with wealth and you were in good standing in the community, God must have looked favorably on you and blessed you. You were successful according to man's standard. If hard times came upon you, then you must have sinned, and God was punishing you for that sin. This is an error. The fact that you have money and wealth does not mean God has looked favorably on you. Money and wealth is not the gauge in which God looks at us. That's how man gauges success. If you have money and wealth, and you are not careful, they can become your master. Remember, you cannot serve two masters. God looks at our heart, our character, not our social standing.

The Israelites were so concerned about what the written word said that they scrutinized it, evaluated it, interpreted it; and after all that, they missed the meaning. They missed Christ, which means

Messiah. Israel, in all of its laws, regulations, rules, dos and don'ts, they missed the part where God sent His Son to save the world. They were His chosen people and should have been the example to everyone in the world. The Jews were to show all humans how to worship God, the Creator of the universe. Jews were so caught up in expecting an earthly king that they missed God's Son when he came the first time. They didn't expect the Messiah to suffer. They expected the Messiah would come in power and put the Israelites in authority, with them leading humanity. It's hard to imagine they missed the fact that God sent His Son. The fact is, they missed seeing the truth, and they crucified the truth: Christ. What a terrible time in the history of humanity when they tried to take the life of God's Son. The world was in tribulation during the birth, childhood, young adulthood, ministry, death on the cross, and the resurrection of Christ.

Christ physical life on earth was short. He touched so many people in so many ways. Only the end will tell the entire story of the greatness that walked among us. Jesus brought peace to a troubled world. This peace that He brought was a peace that no man can take from us. The people were seeking the Messiah to take over as a worldly king and set up an earthly kingdom. Israel was not searching for someone to bring peace in their hearts. They were looking for a physical peace on earth. That's not why Christ came the first time. They were searching for someone to take over their physical state, not their spiritual state. Israel wanted to kick the Romans out of power and set themselves up as the ones with the power, the ones in charge. Power is a very corrupt thing in the lives of men. Man has never been able to handle power; it always seems to corrupt the person that has it. When power is in the mix, good men go astray and do bad things in the name of good. Evil and greed always seem to make good men change. When Christ walked on earth, men were in a sad state of corruption.

Christ's ministry was three and a half years long. He brought peace and hope to a troubled world in those three and a half years. The people were looking for an earthly king, and they got a heavenly king in the flesh. Our peace from God will be with us regard-

CHURCH AGE

less of what is going on around us. We have a peace from God that non-Christians cannot understand.

God knew of man's sinful heart and lack of faithfulness. How could man be trusted to keep the covenant he made with God? God knows everything, and God's love can overcome anything. Man has made the wrong choice after the wrong choice concerning his relationship with God. Jesus Christ has always been the Son of God. Christ is the way out for a lost and dying world. Christ is God's plan to give everyone a way back to Him. Jesus Christ is our personal Savior. We have the choice of spending eternity in heaven with God or eternity in hell with Satan. Your choice. Christ came to show love, not just speak love to the world. Christ came to show how far His unconditional love would reach, and there are no limits to His love.

The church age is in place so that everyone can come to know Jesus Christ. In chapters 2 and 3 of the book of Revelation, it shows these churches with their different weaknesses, strengths, and character. It shows the unique stages the seven churches have to go through.

The Seven Churches of the Church Age

Each letter is addressed to a city and addresses their particular needs of one of the church ages. Each church age will have aspects of the others but specific to their own. How a particular church spelled and pronounced the name depends on the version of your Bible.

King James (KJV)	New King James (NKJV)	New International (NIV)	Modern Language (MLB)	Living Bible (LB)	Revised Standard (RSV)
Ephesus	Ephesus	Ephesus	Ephesus	Ephesus	Ephesus
Smyrna	Smyrna	Smyrna	Smyrna	Smyrna	Smyrna
Pergamos	Pergamos	Pergamum	Pergamum	Pergamos	Pergamum
Thyatira	Thyatira	Thyatira	Thyatira	Thyatira	Thyatira
Sardis	Sardis	Sardis	Sardis	Sardis	Sardis

IS THERE TIME

Phila-	Phila-	Phila-	Phila-	Phila-	Phila-
delphia	delphia	delphia	delphia	delphia	delphia
Laodicea	Laodicean	Laodicea	Laodicea	Laodicea	La-odicea

Chapter 2 and 3 of the book of Revelation give us a breakdown of the seven churches, the names of the seven cities in which the churches were located:

To the angel of the church of Ephesus

To the angel of the church of Smyrna

To the angel of the church of Pergamon

To the angel of the church of Thyatira

To the angel of the church of Sardis

To the angel of the church of Philadelphia

To the angel of the church of Laodicean

The Seven Descriptions of Christ That He Identified
The New King James Version

Ephesus: "He who holds the seven stars in His right hand, who walks in the midst of the seven golden lamp stands."

Smyrna: "The First and the last, who was dead, and came to life."

Pergamos: "He who has the sharp two-edge sword."

Thyatira: "The Son of God, who has eyes like a flame of fire, and His feet like fine brass."

Sardis: "He who has the Spirit of God and the seven stars."

Philadelphia: "He who is holy, He who is true, He who has the key of David, He who opens and no one shuts, and shuts and no one opens."

Laodicean: "The Amen, the Faithful and True Witness, the Beginning of the creation of God."

CHURCH AGE

The Commendation That Jesus Gave to Each Church
New King James Version

Ephesus: "I know your works, your labor, your patience, and that you cannot bear those who are evil, and you tested those who say they are apostles and are not, and have found them liars, I know you have preserved and have patience, and have labored for My name's sake and not became weary."

Smyrna: "I know your works, tribulation, and poverty."

Pergamos: "I know you're works, and where you dwell, where Satan's throne is. And you hold fast to My name, and did not deny My name, and did not deny My faith even in the days in which Antipas was My faithful martyr, who's was killed among you, where Satan dwells."

Thyatira: "I know you're works, love, service, faith, and your patience; and as for your works, the last are more than the first."

Sardis: "I know you're works, that you have a name that you are alive, but you are dead. Be watchful, and strengthen the things which remain, that are ready to die, for I have not found your works perfect before God."

Philadelphia: "I know you're works. See, I set before you an open door, and no one can shut it; for you have a little strength, have kept My word, and have not denied My name."

Laodicean: None

The lack of commendation to Laodicean age should be a wake-up call to all Christians living in this age. We are living in the Laodicean age. It should be no surprise that this is the church age that will go through the Great Tribulation.

The Criticism Jesus Gave to Each Church
The New King James Version

Ephesus: "That you have left your first love."
Smyrna: None

Pergamos: "Because you have there those who hold the doctrine of Balaam, who taught Balak to put a stumbling block before the children of Israel, to eat things sacrificed to idols, and have committed sexual immorality."

Thyatira: "Because you have allowed that woman Jezebel, who calls herself a prophetess, to teach and seduce My servants to commit sexual immorality and eat things sacrificed to idols."

Sardis: "That you have a name that you are alive, but you are dead."

Philadelphia: None

Laodicean: "That you are neither cold or hot. I could wish you were cold or hot. So there, because you are lukewarm, and neither cold or hot. I will vomit you out of My mouth. Because you say, 'I am rich, have become wealthy, and have need of nothing'—and do not know you are wretched, miserable, poor, blind, and naked."

It is important to note that two of the church ages have no criticism against them: the Smyrna and Philadelphia church age. There are special blessings that relate to these church ages and do not apply to other church ages. These blessings are for the ones with no criticism against them because of their work, faith, and willingness to stand up for God.

The Instruction That Jesus Gave to Each Church
The New King James Version

Ephesus: "Repent and do the first work."
Smyrna: "Be faithful until death."
Pergamos: "Repent."
Thyatira: "But hold fast to what you have till I come."
Sardis: "Be watchful; and strengthen the things that remain… Hold fast and repent."
Philadelphia: "Behold, I am coming quickly! Hold fast what you have, that no one may take your crown."
Laodicea: "I council you to buy from Me gold refined in the fire; that you may be rich; and white garments, that you may be

clothed, that the shame of your nakedness may not be revealed; and anoint your eyes with eye salve, that you may see. As many as I love, I rebuke and chasten, be zealous and repent."

The Promises and Blessings to the Churches

Jesus gave promises to each of the seven churches. There are special blessing in two of the church ages: the Smyrna and Philadelphia age. Where it says, "To him who overcomes," is a promise to all Christians that endure to the end. Failure to overcome means a loss of rewards, not salvation.

Ephesus: "He who has an ear, let him hear what the Spirit says to the churches. To him who overcomes I will give to eat from the tree of life, which is in the midst of paradise of God."
Smyrna: This promise is to the Smyrna church. There was no criticism from Jesus.

"Be Faithful until death, and I will give you the crown of Life."
"He who has an ear, let him hear what the Spirit says to the churches. He who overcomes shall not be hurt by the second death."

Pergamo: "He who has an ear, let him hear what the Spirit Says to the churches. To him who overcomes I will give some of the hidden manna to eat. And I will give him, a white stone, and on the stone a new name written which no one knows except him who receives it."
Thyatira: "He who has an ear, let him hear what the Spirit says to the churches."
Sardis: "He who has an ear, let him hear what the Spirit says to the churches."
Philadelphia: This promise is to the Philadelphia church. There was no criticism from Jesus. "Because you have kept My command to persevere, I also will keep you from the hour of trial which shall come upon the whole world, to test those who dwell on the earth."

"He who overcomes, I will make him a pillar in the temple of My God, and he shall go out no more. I will write on him the name of My God and the name of the city of My God, the New Jerusalem, which comes down out of heaven from My God. And I will write on him My new name. He who has an ear, let him hear what the Spirit says to the churches."

Laodicea: "To him who overcomes, I will grant to sit with Me on My throne, as I also overcame and sat down with My Father on His throne. He who has an ear, let him hear what the Spirit says to the churches."

The first blessing to a specific church is to the Smyrna church age. "The crown of life": the crown of life relates to victory. As they live this life of faith without wavering, God will adorn them with a blessed life, a satisfying life. This doesn't mean that they will not have any trials. It means they will be blessed. They will know His assurance and will be satisfied with whatever Christ wants for them.

The second blessing to a specific church is to the Philadelphia church age: "Because you have kept My command to persevere, I will keep you from the hour of trial which shall come upon the whole world. To test those who dwell on the earth." This is the faithful church, close to the Great Tribulation. God will protect the Philadelphia church age from going through the Great Tribulation. The Laodicean church age will go through the seals, then the Great Tribulation, the trumpets, the bowls and the fall of Babylon. The Philadelphia church age will be protected from the Great Tribulation, they will not go through the hour of trial, the Great Tribulation.

In Revelation 3:20–21, placement and attitude of Christ at the end of the church ages. The Laodicean church age is lukewarm. Laodicean's church goes through all the same characteristics of all the other age descriptions but adds another element.

> Behold, I stand at the door and knock. If anyone hears My voice and opens the door, I will come in to him and dine with him, and he with Me. To

CHURCH AGE

> him who overcomes I will grant to sit with Me on
> My throne, as I also overcame and sat down with
> My Father on His throne. (Rev. 3:20–21 NKJV)

Verse 20 and 21 add another element to the Laodicean church. And verse 22 ends the same way all the other churches end: "He who has an ear, let him hear what the Spirit says to the churches" (Rev. 3:22 NKJV) The phrase, "He who has an ear, let him hear what the Spirit says to the churches," is at the end of all the different church age descriptions. The person who opens their heart and hears what the Spirit says will be opening the truth of God's word. This is essential for understanding.

Look at the descriptions of each of the churches:

Ephesus	the loveless church	the church at the beginning of the church age
Smyrna	the persecuted church	the church under persecution
Pergamos	the compromising church	the church settled in the world
Sardis	the dead church	the church is dead, yet having a believing remnant
Philadelphia	the faithful church	the church in revival
Laodicean	the lukewarm church	the church in its final state of apostasy (abandon a pervious loyalty)

Only two of the churches Christ have nothing against. Smyrna was the second, and Philadelphia was the second from the last. The last church age, Laodicean, has a unique statement against it:

"Lukewarm," and "I will vomit you out of My mouth." "Vomit you out." Now that's some powerful language. That doesn't sound like the church will be taken out before the Great Tribulation. More like I will put you through it to see where your faith lines up. Do you stand with Jesus in His love, or do you stand with the world's hate?

In the Laodicean age, it talks about the shame of your nakedness. Do we reveal more of our bodies than we should and think it to be acceptable? What does the Bible say? "That you may be clothed, that the shame of your nakedness may not be revealed…" (Rev. 3:18b NKJV). Look at the way we dress, men or women. Do we reveal our nakedness? Do we show parts of our bodies that should be reserved for our spouses? What about TV, magazines, and the Internet? Do these mediums expose our nakedness? Our eyes see, but we don't see. I believe we have been so indoctrinate to the sin, and we don't give it another thought. God has given us the signs. We need to see the Laodicean age as it unfolds around us. I wonder just how close are we to the Great Tribulation. Are the signs there, and we just don't acknowledge them? I believe the world has indoctrinated us, and we rationalize sin away and don't see sin for what it is. That is how we sin and don't realize we are even sinning. *Rationalize*: one of the world's favorite words. Do we even know the signs we are to be looking for? "Watch and do not fall asleep." God has given us the signs that we are to be looking for. We need to be opening the Bible, and reading it. Hint! The last book is full of signs. Perhaps it is a book in the Bible that we should think about reading and studying. Remember, anytime you read and study the Bible, bathe it in prayer every step of the way.

The attitudes of these seven churches reflects the different parts of the church age as the church goes through time. The gathering of the Jews to their homeland and making them a nation, 1948, this happened at the end of the Philadelphia age. We will see the second coming of Jesus Christ at the end of the Laodicea church age, at the conclusion of the Great Tribulation.

> Now I saw heaven opened, and behold, a white horse. And He who sat on him was called Faithful

and True, and in righteousness He judges and makes war. His eyes were like a flame of fire, and on His head were many crowns. He had a name written that no one knew except Himself. He was clothed with a robe dipped in blood, and His name is called The Word of God. And the armies in heaven, clothed in fine linen, white and clean, followed Him on white horses. Now out of His mouth goes a sharp sword, that with it He should strike the nations. And He Himself will rule them with a rod of iron. He Himself treads the winepress of the fierceness and wrath of Almighty God. And He has on His robe and on His thigh a name written: KING OF KINGS AND LORD OF LORDS. (Rev. 19:11–16 NKJV)

The rapture of the church comes at Christ's return. This will happen when the Lord returns for His children at the end of the Great Tribulation. The dead in Christ are first, and then we who are alive will be caught up to meet Jesus in the air. From that moment on, we will always be with our Lord.

But I do not want you to be ignorant, brethren, concerning those who have fallen asleep, least you sorrow as others who have no hope. For if we believe that Jesus died and rose again, even so God will bring with Him those who sleep in Jesus. For this we say to you by the word of the Lord, that we who are alive and remain until the coming of the Lord will by no means precede those who are asleep. For the Lord Himself will descend from heaven with a shout, with the voice of an archangel, and with the trumpet of God. And the dead in Christ will rise first. Then we who are alive and remain shall be caught up together with them in the clouds to meet the

> Lord in the air. And thus we shall always be with
> the Lord. Therefore comfort one another with
> these words. (1 Thess. 4:13–18 NKJV)

The book of Revelation reveals Jesus Christ as God's Son, the Savior of the world. As the Laodicean church age takes place, we will see smaller churches disappear and large churches will become larger. The churches focus is on large numbers, larger debt, and big beautiful buildings. When these churches grow in numbers, most of the numbers don't come from new converts. They come from people transferring their membership from other churches. Several of the new converts that do take place will stay as baby Christians, not growing into maturity.

Individuals will give financial support and not be involved physically in the ministry. This way they can feel that they are a part of reaching the lost without ever sharing the good news of Jesus Christ with anyone. The congregation will become more concerned about the status quo instead of the needs of the people. Congregations hire staff to organize, plan, and share Christ. They are so large that they lose their individuality. Large churches will always need volunteers, and they cannot function without them. The megachurch philosophy plays into people getting lost in church not having to get involved, but they are present and this makes them feel good. The one-world church will begin during the Laodicea church age. The church age will end when Christ returns: "He will descend from heaven with a shout, with the voice of an archangel, and with the trumpet of God." This is the trumpet that is talked about for the rapture; it is when Christ returns.

CHAPTER 10

Tribulation, End-Time Tribulation, Great Tribulation

WHAT IS TRIBULATION? HUMANS ARE distressed and suffering from oppression. Before Jesus and the cross, there was Tribulation; and after Jesus and the cross, there is End-Time Tribulation. End-Time Tribulation: people are being persecuted because of Jesus, to stop them from believing and following Him. The End-Time Tribulation ends with the seals. The Great Tribulation will be the worst persecution the world has ever seen. It will fall on everyone, but the focus will be on Christians. It will start with the trumpets and continue until Christ's return. They are judgments on earth and its inhabitants. The beast being loosed is the last of the three woes.

The First woe: locusts from the bottomless pit. They had tails like scorpions. Their power was to hurt men for five months.
The Second woe: the four angels rode horses with heads like lions. Out of their mouths came fire, smoke, and brimstone. By these three plagues, a third of mankind was killed, and their tails were like serpents, having heads to do harm.
The Third woe: the great dragon, that serpent of old, called the devil and Satan, was cast out of heaven with his angels to earth. Before the trumpets were the seals, which are the warning signs

that people should look for. Then the trumpets, bowls, and the fall of Babylon. The people and the earth is judged.

Tribulation has always been among us in one form or another. The End-Time Tribulation starts with Christ coming for the first time and ends when the seals conclude. The Great Tribulation starts with the Trumpets and ends when Christ returns.

The End-Time Tribulation ends with the seals. The signs we are to be looking for are in the seals:

First Seal	The conqueror, the white horse; Antichrist trying to look like Christ, his bow indicates warrior, his crown represents power and or ruler.
Second Seal	Conflict on earth, war, the red horse; they took peace from the earth. There was no peace anywhere on earth, and people killed one another.
Third Seal	Famine, the black horse; food became very scarce on earth.
Fourth Seal	Death on earth, the pale horse; the rider was death and Hades and he has power over a fourth of the earth. They killed with sword, with hunger, and with the beast of the earth.
Fifth Seal	Cry of the martyrs: the martyrs who were slain for the word of God, they cry out to the Lord, "How long, oh Lord!"
Sixth Seal	Cosmic disturbances; a great earthquake; the sun became black; the moon became like blood; the stars fall to earth, every mountain and island moved out of its place; every king, great men, rich men, mighty men, every slave, and free man hide in the caves of the mountains.
Seventh Seal	Prepare the seven trumpets

TRIBULATION, END-TIME TRIBULATION, GREAT TRIBULATION

The white horse means he was trying to pass himself off as Christ. The crown means he had some kind of authority. Going out to conquer means he will set up a worldly empire to rule the inhabitants of the world.

Between the seventh seal and the first trumpet, there is silence in heaven for a half hour. There were seven angels, and they had seven trumpets, and the seven angels prepare to sound the trumpets.

The Great Tribulation will come when the trumpets start. Trumpets are where God sends angels against vegetation, seas, the heavens (moon and stars), and the three woes. Seals are the warning signs that the Great Tribulation is coming.

The earth is always in some kind of persecution/tribulation in some part of the world. Communication heightens the awareness, and this is globally and instantly. When the trumpets start, this persecution is on a bigger scale, more intense. We see the term *great* beginning to be used.

> And something like a *great* mountain burning with fire was thrown into the sea, and a third of the sea became blood. (Rev. 8:8 NKJV)

> Then the third angel sounded: And a *great* star fell from heaven, burning like a torch, and it fell on a third of the rivers and on the springs of water. (Rev. 8:10 NKJV)

> So the *great* dragon was cast out, that serpent of old, called the Devil and Satan, who deceives the whole world; he was cast to the earth, and his angels were cast out with him. (Rev. 12:9 NKJV)

> Therefore rejoice, O heavens, and you who dwell in them! Woe to the inhabitants of the earth and the seas! For the devil has come down to you, having *great* wrath, because he knows that he has a short time. (Rev. 12:12 NKJV)

> And he was given a mouth speaking *great* things and blasphemies, and was given authority to continue for forty-two months. (Rev. 13:5 NKJV)

Satan was given authority for three and a half years. Now things have changed. Satan has authority here on earth.

The first of the seven trumpets will begin with the Great Tribulation. God will strike the vegetation, seas, waters, and then the three woes. These are judgments and a warning to repent. For those who do not have their name in the book of life, the outcome is not good. Satan is removed from heaven, this is the final of three woes. Satan is cast down to earth and never again allowed to return to heaven.

> It was granted to him to make war with the saints and to overcome them. And authority was given him over every tribe, tongue, and nation. (Rev. 13:7 NKJV)

> And I looked, and I heard an angel flying through the midst of heaven, saying with a loud voice, "Woe, woe, woe to the inhabitants of the earth, because of the remaining blasts of the trumpet of the three angels who are about to sound!" (Rev. 8:13 NKJV)

In the Great Tribulation, Satan speaks blasphemies against God and anything related to God. Satan seeks to destroy and make war on the saints of God. All who dwell on the earth will worship Satan, except the ones who have their name written in the Book of Life. After Revelation chapter 3, there is no use of the term *church*. It does uses the term *saints*. After the cross and until Christ's return, anyone who is saved is a part of the church. Terms used to describe believing Christians in all of the church ages: *believers in Christ, followers of Christ*, the *bride of Christ, saints*, and the *church*.

TRIBULATION, END-TIME TRIBULATION, GREAT TRIBULATION

Many things will happen. Many signs will appear to wake up the lukewarm church and bring them back to God. God always provides a way for men to return to Him, but the choice is theirs. Man has to take a step of faith to receive what God has provided. God is a just and fair God and wants no one to be lost, but will not force humans to make the right decision. At the end of the End-Time Tribulation, it is no accident that the last church age is lukewarm. In this age, the church will not stand up against the things that Satan and his demons start to do. The church is wealthy and thinks that they need God, but does not depend on Him for their needs. They are big and self-sufficient. They will claim to be doing God's work, doing so many things and staying so busy but missing the Christ relationship.

This age is a lot like the time the Pharisees and the Sadducees made so many rules and regulations. They looked like God's servants outwardly, appearing to do His work. God does not look at the things we have and do but at the heart, the attitude in which we do them. The church is so indifferent to what is going on in the world during the Laodicea age. They see but not with clarity. It's blurred. Besides, they are so busy doing things that look good and that don't affect the lost for Christ, so Satan is not attacking them. Satan is cunning, and he will strike. He is setting the stage for what is going to happen. Are we listening to Christ, or are we becoming masters at rationalizing sin away? The Laodicean age bring new definition to rationalizing sin away. Do we take a stand for Christ, or do we not want to upset the status quo?

In the book of Revelation, the Laodicea church doesn't talk about what they did right. It says they are lukewarm, neither cold nor hot. He will vomit them out of His mouth. This church age is wealthy and needs little. It looks to how people can solve things rather than God to solve them. They will become so self-sufficient and *not* reliant on God. The church looks at having things that the world considers good and right, like big beautiful buildings and men remembering men more than God. Man and the things that he accomplishes will become the focus instead of God being the focus.

IS THERE TIME

In Matthew, Mark, and Luke, they all give you an account of the order in that things will happen at the end. They say it a little different but basically the same thing. Any of the three would be good to go through. I am going to use Mark for this:

The destruction of the temple: He tells His disciples to look at these building, not one stone will remain standing upon another. It talks about signs in Matthew 24, Mark 13, and Luke 21.

Then as He went out of the temple, one of His disciples said to Him, "Teacher, see what manner of stones and what buildings are here!" And Jesus said to him, "Do you see these great buildings? Not one stone shall be left upon another, that shall not be thrown down" (Mark 13:1–2 NKJV).

Signs of the end times: this tells of things to look for that will happen in the future. How far in the future no one knows, but there are signs for us to look for.

> Now as He sat on the Mount of Olives opposite the temple, Peter, James, John, and Andrew asks Him privately, "Tell us, when will these things be? And what will be the sign when all these things will be fulfilled?"
>
> And Jesus, answering them, began to say: "Take heed that no one deceives you. For many will come in My name, saying, 'I am He,' and will deceive many. But when you hear of wars and rumors of wars, do not be troubled; for such things must happen, but the end is not yet. For nation will rise against nation, and kingdom against kingdom. And there will be earthquakes in various places, and there will be famines and troubles. These are the beginnings of sorrows."
> (Mark 13:1–2 NKJV)

The church age ends at the end of the Great Tribulation.

We will need to pay close attention to our surroundings. We can be given up to the law and punished and in the process be hurt

TRIBULATION, END-TIME TRIBULATION, GREAT TRIBULATION

and beaten. You and I will be taken before the people who are in charge and accused of being a follower of Christ, and that testimony will be what gets us in trouble. Every one of us must share the Gospel with everyone. When we are arrested and brought before a judge, don't worry about what you will say. The Holy Spirit will give you the words to say. On that day, brother will be against brother, father will turn on his children, and children against their father. Children will rise against their parents, and death will be the outcome. We will be hated because of the name of Jesus Christ. We are to endure to the end.

When we see the things talked about in Daniel, the abomination standing where it should not be, all men should flee and just take what is on their back. Don't go back for anything. Hurry and get to a safe place if you can find one. The great tribulation will be the worst the world has ever seen.

When these things take place, you will see people pretending to be Christ; know that they are not Christ. False Christ and the false prophets will come with signs and wonders, all fake, trying to deceive you. But know that Christ has warned us about these things. Reference to Mark 13:3–13.

Christ Is Returning for His Church!

At the end of the Great Tribulation, Jesus Christ is returning. Christ returns for the chosen and the faithful. The chosen is God's chosen people, the Israelites who have believed in Christ as there Savior that makes them a part of the church. The faithful is the church.

> But in those days, after that tribulation, the sun will be darkened, and the moon will not give its light; the stars of heaven will fall, the powers in the heavens will be shaken. Then they will see the Son of Man coming in the clouds with great power and glory. And then He will send His angels, and gather together His elect from the four winds,

from the farthest part of the earth to the farthest part of heaven. (Mark 13:24–27 NKJV)

Also in Matthew 24:29–31 and Luke 21:25–28.

What do you need to be a Christian? It is not what you know about Christ; it is your relationship with Him. Christ delivers us from our sins. He is our Savior. He is our salvation. He is the Son of God, Jesus Christ.
The question was, what do you need to be a Christian?
The answer is the Son of God, Jesus Christ.
What is salvation?

- It is the gospel message.
- It is the power of God to save everyone.
- It is the preaching of the gospel that has its power to free and rescue people from their sins.
- It is Christ's sacrificial death on the cross in place of all sinners. He is the author and provider of salvation.

The word *salvation* used by Paul in Romans means deliverance.

> For I am not ashamed of the gospel of Christ, for it is the power of God to salvation for everyone who believes, for the Jew first and also for the Greek. (Rom. 1:16 NKJV)

> Let it be known to you all, and to all the people of Israel, that by the name of Jesus Christ of Nazareth, whom you crucified, whom God raised from the dead, by Him this man stands here before you whole. This is the 'stone which was rejected by you builders, which has become the chief cornerstone.' Nor is there salvation in any other, for there is no other name under

heaven given among men by which we must be saved. (Acts 4:10–12 NKJV)

God offers spiritual deliverance to all. They must repent and trust in Jesus to experience this blessing.

For by grace you have been saved through faith, and that not of yourselves; it is a gift of God, not of works, lest anyone should boast. (Eph. 2:8–9 NKJV)

What are those blessings?

Salvation from the penalty of sin: Jesus paid the price for our sins. We no longer have to pay the price.
Salvation from the power of sin: He delivers us from the power of sin, and we have the Holy Spirit to aid us in our journey.
Salvation from the presence of sin: there will be a time when we will be with the Father and there will be no more sin anywhere! Amen!

To survive tribulation, we need to understand three terms that relate to salvation. They are *justification, sanctification,* and *glorification.*

Justification is the divine act of declaring sinners to be righteous because of their faith in Jesus Christ.

Therefore, having been justified by faith, we have peace with God through our Lord Jesus Christ. (Rom. 5:1 NKJV)

God has caused our sins to go away as far as the east is from the west. Our sins are no more. They are gone forever. We are a new creature in Jesus Christ. Sin no longer holds us hostage. When we become a child of God, we inherit the kingdom of God. We become a part of the promise God made to Abraham. God adopts each of us into his family, and we become His children. We are justified by faith in Jesus Christ. He is the one who paid the price for our sin. The justification that He gives us makes us one of His children. No one can take us out of our Father's hand. We will be His child forever.

Sanctification is the process that God develops in us. It is the new life of a believer and brings it gradually into perfection.

> Being confident of this very thing, that he who has begun a good work in you will complete it until the day of Jesus Christ. (Phil. 1:6 NKJV)

Christ sanctifies each of us by removing our sin, layer by layer. God replaces our sin with His love and grace. He died for us once and thus justified us into His family. Once we became His child, we are His forever. No man, no woman, no one can take us out of His grace. As we stumble and learn what it means to be a Christian, this is where sanctification comes in. We need to be obedient and ask for forgiveness of our sins, and He will forgive us. Because He loves us, the Father will correct us as we go on our journey. We will grow to have a closer walk with Christ as He molds and makes us into the person we were created to be. We lose some of our sinful walk and start a Christlike walk. As long as there is a sin nature we have to contend with, we will have growing pains. It's making one clean as we grow in the Lord and walk in the paths of the Lord.

We stumble and fall as we go on our journey. He lovingly picks us up and makes us clean as we take this journey. The more He cleans us, the more we resemble Jesus. As we go through the cleaning process, the darkness starts to lose its appeal, and the light becomes our desire more and more. As we stumble, the Holy Spirit will teach and change us a little with each step. It takes a lifetime of molding and shaping us to get us where God wants and intended for us to be. We need more of Jesus in control of our lives and less of our sinful nature.

More of you, Lord, and less of me.

TRIBULATION, END-TIME TRIBULATION, GREAT TRIBULATION

Glorification is the ultimate salvation of the whole person.

> For our citizenship is in heaven, from which we also eagerly wait for the Savior, the Lord Jesus Christ, who will transform our lowly body that it may be conformed to His glorious body, according to the working by which He is able even to subdue all things to Himself. (Phil. 3:20–21 NKJV)

The idea is to rescue us from the power and dominion of sin.

Example: a man married a woman and they had a child. As the child grew, the child chose to disobey his parents, even disrespect one or both of them. Does the father disown the child? No. The father will always love the child, and he is a part of the family no matter what. We love the person not the sin. How many times does the father forgive the child? How many times does he give grace to his child? He will forgive and show grace as often as needed to restore the fellowship within the family. God the Father or human father raising a family, they both desire to have fellowship with their children. Neither one will tolerate the disobedience, sin, but both will love their children forever. Amen!

2 Corinthians 12:9 (NKJV)	My grace is sufficient for you, for My strength is made perfect in weakness.
Titus 2:11 (NKJV)	For the grace of God that brings salvation has appeared to all men.
2 Corinthians 13:14 (NKJV)	The grace of the Lord Jesus Christ, and the love of God, and the communion of the Holy Spirit be with you all. Amen.

IS THERE TIME

Tribulation age is before Christ, the time of the Jews. The End-Time Tribulation is after Christ, the time of the Gentiles. The Great Tribulation is after the seals until Christ's return.

Chapter 11

The Rapture

When you talk about the rapture, it all comes down to your point of view and your interpretation of Scripture. It is not cut and dry or black and white. The rapture, the caught up, is when the dead in Christ will be raised first, then the saints who are alive at Christ's return go and meet Him in the air. Before Christ's return, every person will have heard the message of Jesus Christ's love and God's plan of salvation for them.

Where do the saints that have passed on go before the new heaven and the new earth are in place? Before Christ, they sleep in the Lord, and after Christ, they will be placed into a temporary body that God has prepared for us. From this heaven, you will be able to see the earth and the place God has prepared for the ones who are not saints of God. There is a span between the three places, and no one can travel between them. We will recognize the ones that have gone before us to heaven. This place that God has prepared for us, our friends, and our loved ones. This heaven will be glorious, beyond what we can imagine. Saints will be able to see what is happening on earth and in the place prepared for unbelievers. They cannot interfere with anything that is going on. They will only be able to offer prayers. God and Christ will permeate the heaven. It will be a place of great joy and praising God. Christ has gone ahead of us to prepare a place for each of His followers for when we leave for heaven. There are three phases that our bodies will go through: the body we now hold, a temporary body God has prepared for each of us, and the final body will be a body transformed into what we will have for eternity. We will maintain our individuality of what makes us unique in the Lord as a person. But know this: whatever happens, God will change our bodies for the better.

There are three heavens. The first heaven was when God created the earth and placed a garden in it. The second heaven is a temporary place where Christians go when they leave this body we now use. The final heaven will be when the new heaven and the new earth are put in their final place. This place is a place of great joy, peace, and no sin. Heaven is, and will be, a very real and tangible place.

Hell is a very real and tangible place. Hell is a place for people who did not follow God and don't know Christ as their personal Savior. They have a place prepared for them as well. Being a good person is not good enough. It will *not* get you into heaven; it only gets you into hell. There are two places. The first place is for an unbeliever that does not have a personal relationship with Christ. Death and Hades will hold the ones who don't believe before Christ. The second place is a temporary place. They will be able to see the earth and the temporary heaven. It will be a place you don't want to go too. There will be a gulf between the two places, and they cannot pass from one place to the other. The third and final place is the place that Satan will be cast into and bound to forever. This place is for anyone who followed Satan and the ones whose name are not found in the Book of Life. In this place, there is no joy or peace, only pain and suffering. The pain will not cease; the burning will continue forever. Whoever is placed there will literality feel this pain. The pain will not be numbing after a while. There will be no relief, forever! Most of us have at one time or the other burned our hand by touching a hot item. That doesn't feel good. Have you ever seen a person where they are burned so badly he or she has to go to a burn center? If you want to know what hell will be like, look that up. It will bring new meaning to your definition of pain. I have never heard of one person that went through that and wanted to go through it a second time.

THE RAPTURE

Hell will be many times worse than that could ever be, and you never get over that pain because it never stops. There is nothing you can do to stop the pain. If you don't know Christ as your Savior, hell is your destination for eternity. Once you are there, there is no do over. You are there for eternity.

If we look back in the history of man where God is dealing with His creation, God has never taken His people out of the tribulation they were enduring. He saw them through the tribulation. Their faith was tested. Words were not enough, and their actions spoke to the true nature of their heart, what they believed. To be a Christian, attending a local church is not a place to make business connections, to be in the accepted status quo. When things are more important than sharing Christ and advancing His kingdom, there is a problem. We read about the different church ages, and it gives us a good look at what God sees in His creation. Many people look for the rapture of the church to be before the great tribulation. When you read about the last church age, Laodicean, I have a hard time finding a reason God would take the church out before the Great Tribulation. In Revelation, it talks about the Laodicean church age, the last church age. This is what God thinks about the last church age:

> I know your works, that you are neither cold nor hot. I could wish you were cold or hot. So then, because you are lukewarm, and neither cold nor hot, I will vomit you out of My mouth. Because you say, "I am rich, have become wealthy, and have need of nothin" and do not know that you are wretched, miserable, poor, blind, and naked—I counsel you to buy from Me gold refined in the fire, that you may be rich; and white garments, that you may be clothed, that your shame of your nakedness may not be revealed; and anoint your eyes with eye salve, that you may see. As many as I love, I rebuke and chasten. Therefore be zealous and repent. (Rev. 3:15–19 NKJV)

IS THERE TIME

American is the land of the blessed, because of what our fathers did and believed. This nation is changing, and not for the better. Our nation is advancing one's personal rights. People are advancing self instead God. Personal rights have replaced right and wrong. God has blessed this nation from its beginnings, because we acknowledged that God is the one who gave us this freedom we now enjoy. God can take this away as quickly as He gave it to us. People think this nation is great because of what we have done without help from a higher, unseen force. Individuals turn their back on God and declare that they no longer need Him, and they worship the one who deceives them. He will chastise us one day for this. All you have to do is look around, and you can tell Satan is at work and alive and well.

Christ's return is at the end the Great Tribulation. Many people think that the church is something other than the people. The church is not the building. The building is where the church meets. Christ's church is the people that believe in Jesus Christ as there Savior. Christ is there King, Lord of their life, the Messiah. There will be Christians during the Great Tribulation until the end when Christ returns. During that time, Christians will have to show their faith, stand up for Christ, if needed, lay down their life.

> Let us be glad and rejoice and give Him glory, for
> the marriage of the Lamb has come, and His wife
> has made herself ready. (Rev. 19:7 NKJV)

The church is the bride of Christ, and Christ is the lamb. Revelation describes the church ages in chapter 2 and 3. This tell of the past, present, and the future. Revelation 4:1 to 19:11 tells us of the things in the future, terrifying events: End Time and Great Tribulation. In Revelation 7, it talks about the Jews and the Gentiles saved during the Great Tribulation. This End-Time Tribulation was going on in John's day as the early church was starting. The End-Time Tribulation will go on during the last of the church ages takes place. The last church age is the Laodicean age, which is lukewarm. Christ brought an inner peace to all Christians during the persecu-

THE RAPTURE

tion going on all around Him. The church age was put into place to reach the world. God wants all to come to know His saving grace.

End-Time Tribulation that is talked about in Revelation 4:1 to 6:17. The 144,000 of all the tribes of the children of Israel were sealed is talked about in Revelation 7:1 to 7:8. The Christian multitude coming out from the End-Time Tribulation is talked about in Revelation 7:9 to 7:17. Seventh seal, the trumpets announce the war that is talked about in Revelation 8:1 to 11:19. God wages war on evil.

The question is, Is anyone that is saved after the cross to the return of Christ spoken of in 1 Thessalonians 4:14–17 part of the church, and will they be a part of the marriage of Christ? A better question might be, If the rapture happens before the Great Tribulation, before Christ return and the church is removed, that would mean there are no Christians at this point on earth. If Christ takes His light out of the world, who will tell the remaining people on earth about Christ's love? In Revelation 18:23, the seals, the trumpets, and the bowls have happened; and God is getting ready to judge Babylon. It says, "The light of a lamp shall not shine in you anymore, and the voice of the bridegroom and the bride shall not be heard in you anymore…" (Rev. 18:23a NKJV). The light of the world are Christians: "For you were once darkness, but now you are light in the Lord. Walk as children of light…" (Eph. 5:8 NKJV).

Christ is living through each of us, and His light will shine through us to the world. In Revelation 18:23, Christ is getting ready to remove His light, and it will not shine there anymore. The term *church* is not used after chapter 3 of Revelation. When the rapture happens, all Christians, believers in Christ, will go to be with Him forever! There will not be any of the church left behind. All the church gets to go. When we become a Christian, we become a member of the church. Our hope is found in scripture. The rapture happens when Christ returns. His return is *not* before the Great Tribulation.

> For if we believe that Jesus died and rose again, even so God will bring with Him those who sleep in Jesus. For this we say to you by the word of

> the Lord, that we who are alive and remain until the coming of the Lord will by no means precede those who are asleep. For the Lord Himself will descend from heaven with a shout, with the voice of an archangel, and with the trumpet of God. And the dead in Christ will rise first. Then we who are alive and remain shall be caught up together with them in the clouds to meet the Lord in the air. And thus we shall always be with the Lord. (1 Thess. 4:14–17 NKJV)

Paul was a part of the church age. And 1 Thessalonians 4:15 says *we* when referring to believers. The time when the rapture will take place is "we who are alive and remain until the coming of the Lord." Verse 15 tells us a lot about the rapture (caught up). "We who are alive." The use of the word *we* encompass Christians in Paul's time, in our time, and in the future. However long or short that will be, no one knows. Christ walked among men, died on the cross, rose from the dead victorious. At the return of Christ, we meet Him in the air. "And remain," all who stay until a certain time "until the coming of the Lord." The coming of the Lord is found in Revelation 19:11–16. The seals, trumpets, bowls, and the judgment of Babylon happens in Revelations 6:1 to 18:24. Revelation 18:23, the light is going to be removed. The church is the light. In Revelations 19:7, it says, "The marriage of the Lamb has come, and His wife has made herself ready." Christ returns in Revelations 19:11–16, "The Lord Himself will descend from heaven with a shout." When the Lord returns in the clouds, the ones who are alive will meet Him in the clouds, but not before the ones who are asleep in Christ. The rapture of the church will be at Christ's return, and then we will be with Him forever.

> In a moment, in the twinkling of an eye, at the last trumpet. For the trumpet will sound, and the dead will be raised incorruptible, and shall be changed. For this corruptible must put on incor-

THE RAPTURE

ruption, and this mortal must put on immortality. (1 Cor. 15:52–53 NKJV)

Some think that this puts the rapture at the end of the seals and beginning of the trumpets. Others think this puts the rapture at the end of the trumpets and the beginning of the bowls. It isn't announcing one of God's judgments on earth and man.

> For the Lord Himself will descend from heaven with a shout, with the voice of an archangel, and with the trumpet of God. And the dead in Christ will rise first. Then we who are alive and remain shall be caught up together with them in the clouds to meet the Lord in the air. And thus we shall always be with the Lord. (1 Thess. 4:16–17 NKJV)

Revelation tells us of Christ's return.

John saw heaven open, and there was a white horse. The one who was on the white horse was called Faithful and True. He judges in righteousness and makes war. His eyes were like a fire, and he had many crowns. No one knew his name but himself. He was wearing a robe dipped in blood. His name was called The Word of God. His armies followed him on white horses. A sharp sword came out of his mouth and could strike all nations. He rules with a rod of iron. He would tread the winepress, the fierceness and wrath of God Almighty. And on his robe and thigh was a name: King of kings and Lord of lords. Reference to Revelation 19:11–16.

This is after the seals, the trumpets, the bowls, and the judgment of Babylon.

Believers that are alive are to watch for His return.

> Behold, I am coming as a thief. Blessed is he who watches, and keeps his garments, lest he walk naked and they see his shame. (Rev. 16:15 NKJV)

IS THERE TIME

Revelation 3:10 talks about the church that was faithful, the Philadelphia church age: "Will keep you from the hour of trial..." Some think that this promise refers to the rapture of the church before the Great Tribulation occurs. While others think it means that the believers of the Philadelphia age will be protected from the hour of trial, the Great Tribulation. The Philadelphia church age is what this is talking about. The Philadelphia church age will not see the Great Tribulation because it was the faithful church. This was their reward. The Great Tribulation will happen after the people of the Philadelphia church age have gone to be with the Lord.

Will people be willing to stand on their faith in the face of their freedom? How much will you be willing to offer the Lord? If the Lord required your house or car, your life, husband or wife, son or daughter, granddaughter or grandson, would you be willing to give for our Lord? Christians, this takes on a completely new meaning during the Great Tribulation or does it for you? How much do you love the Lord? What do you think Satan will use on you to get you to deny Christ? How much did Christ pay for you?

> Now it came to pass after these things that God tested Abraham, and said to Him, "Abraham!" And he said, "Here am I" Then he said, "Take now your son, your only son Isaac, whom you love, and go to the land of Moriah, and offer him there as a burnt offering on one of the mountains of which I shall tell you." (Gen. 22:1–2 NKJV)

Back as far as time has any record, you see that Christians have *never* been removed out of the persecution that they were going through. It was a time to test and show their faith, and God would see them through the hardship. In 2 Timothy 3, it talks about perilous times for men of God.

In the last days, these are the signs that you can look for men and women will be: lovers of themselves, lovers of money, boaster, proud, say evil against God, disobedient to parents, unthankful, unholy, unloving, unforgiving, slanders, brutal, without self-control, despisers of good, traitor, headstrong, haughty, lovers of pleasure rather than lovers of God and having a form of godliness but denying its power. Reference to 2 Timothy 3:1–5.

Individuals with these traits are people we should not associate with. These type of people ease into the households of ones who have all kinds of gullible men and women that are loaded down with sins in their lives. People with these traits resist the truth. They are men and women with corrupt minds. They disapprove of our faith.

Christians who follow His doctrine will have purpose, faith, long-suffering, love, perseverance, persecution, and afflictions. And from these, the Lord will deliver us. All who choose to live godly lives in Christ will suffer persecution. Evil imposters will become worse in the last days and deceive many. Continue in what you have learned from childhood, the Scriptures, which show us salvation through faith in the Lord Jesus Christ. Reference to 2 Timothy 3:1–17.

God's purpose in the church is to raise coheirs who will share Christ's authority in His kingdom. We must overcome as Christ overcame, despite suffering.

> To him who overcomes I will grant to sit with Me on My throne, as I also overcame and sat down with My Father on His throne. (Rev. 3:21 NKJV)

> And if children, then heirs-heirs of God and joint heirs with Christ, if indeed we suffer with Him, that we may also be glorified together. (Rom. 8:17 NKJV)

> If we endure, we shall also reign with Him. If we deny Him, He will also deny us. (2 Tim. 2:12 NKJV)

Many believe that where it says, "Come up here" used in Revelation 4:1 is calling the church to be raptured before the Great Tribulation starts. This was John who went up to heaven to see not the church being raptured.

IS THERE TIME

John is talking.

> After these things I looked, and behold, a door standing open in heaven. And the first voice which I heard was like a trumpet speaking with me, saying, "come up here, and I will show you things which must take place after this." Immediately I was in the Spirit; and behold, a throne set in heaven, and One sat on the throne. (Rev. 4:1–2 NKJV)

> After this I looked, and, behold, a door was opened in heaven: and the first voice which I heard was as it were of a trumpet talking with me; which said, Come up hither, and I will shew thee things which must be hereafter. And immediately I was in the spirit: and, behold, a throne was set in heaven, and one sat on the throne. (Rev. 4:1–2 KJV)

> After this I looked, and there before me was a door standing open in heaven. And the voice I had first heard speaking to me like a trumpet said, "Come up here, and I will show you what must take place after this." At once I was in the Spirit, and there before me was a throne in heaven with someone setting on it. (Rev. 4:1–2 NIV)

Twenty-four elders occupy thrones. Some think that the elders represent the church, believers in heaven.

> Around the throne were twenty-four thrones, and on the thrones I saw twenty-four elders setting, clothed in white robes; and they had crowns of gold on their heads. (Rev. 4:4 NKJV)

THE RAPTURE

Some people think these elders represent angels who comprise a heavenly ruling council. These elders function as ruling priest in the present age. Michael, an angel, identified as one of the chief princes in Daniel.

> But the prince of the kingdom of Persia withstood me twenty-one days; and behold, Michael, one of the chief princes, came to help me, for I had been left alone there with the kings of Persia. (Dan. 10:13 NKJV)

The church will end the same way it began: in a time of great persecution. In the beginning of the church, Christian lives were given to further the cause of Christ. In Acts 5:41, it tells us that the apostles thought it worthy to suffer for the name of Christ. This was during server persecution. During the Great Tribulation, Christians will suffer the same as when Christ walked on earth. Christian's lives will be given to further the cause of Christ. People are lured into a false sense of security. We need to remember we are soldiers in the army of God. When Christ returns, every eye shall see this event.

The day of the Lord in the Old Testament was shown in two ways: God's judgment on sinful people and God's eternal reign over His people. In the New Testament, there will be the great white throne judgment. Christians will experience the resurrection and will not have to take part in the great white throne judgment. At the great white throne judgment, anyone not found in the Book of Life is cast into the lake of fire.

> Then I saw a great white throne and Him who sat on it, from whose face the earth and heaven fled away. And there was found no place for them. And I saw the dead, small and great, standing before God, and books were opened. And another book was opened, which is the Book of Life. And the dead were judged according to their works, by the things which were written in the books. The

> sea gave up the dead who were in it, and Death and Hates delivered the dead who were in them. And they were judged, each one according to his works. Then Death and Hades were cast into the lake of fire. This is the second death. And anyone not found written in the Book of Life was cast into the lake of fire. (Rev. 20:11–15 NKJV)

The New Testament didn't come to replace the Old Testament but to fulfill the Old Testament.

Did God take His people out of the tribulation going on around them? No! It will be the same in the Great Tribulation. It is clear that Christians will not have a part in the second death, eternal pain, torment, and separation from God. We will be with Christ forever, never to be separated.

> For God did not appoint us to wrath, but to obtain salvation through our Lord Jesus Christ. (1 Thess. 5:9 NKJV)

> For God did not appoint us to suffer wrath but to receive salvation through our Lord Jesus Christ. (1 Thess. 5:9 NIV)

Christ will protect Christians from the wrath of the second resurrection. They will be with God forever. They will not have to be a part of eternal separation from God. The wrath of the second judgment will not affect us. We will be a part of the first judgment. His mercy and grace are our reward because we personally know our Lord and Savior, Jesus Christ. This part in Thessalonians is talking about the day when the Lord returns. In the second judgment, no Christian will have to partake of His wrath, judgment. God's wrath and judgment are complete in the second death. God will cast the ones not found in the book of life into the lake of fire, which has a flame that will never go out.

THE RAPTURE

> What is wrath? Wrath is anger, vengeance, punishment, and judgment.

Wrath: strong vengeful anger or indignation, retributory punishment for an offense or a crime, divine chastisement, a divine judgment inflected on a deserving offender
Anger: a strong feeling of annoyance, displeasure, hostility, rage, irritation, indignation, fury
Vengeance: punishment inflicted in retaliation for an injury or offense
Punishment: suffering, pain, or loss that serves as retribution, a penalty inflicted on an offender through judicial procedure
Judgment: the capacity to assess situations or circumstances shrewdly and to draw sound conclusions

God's finial judgment of the second death is on all who are unbelievers, ones who are not a part of Christ's church.

The rapture (caught up) will happen when the Lord returns. When Christ returns to take His church, people will not wonder what happened. Everyone will see this event. From that moment on, we will be with the Lord.

> Behold, He is coming with clouds, and every eye will see Him, even they who pierced Him. And all the tribes of the earth will mourn because of Him. Even so, Amen. (Rev. 1:7 NKJV)

Some say that the Great Tribulation will only be for the Jews and not for the Gentiles. Jews and Gentiles, upon acceptance of Jesus, we become a part of God's family. When the rapture happens, will God separate His family? He will not. The Laodicea church age is disobedient to God.

Christ will return for His church. The church is made up of Jews and Gentiles. To become a part of the church, it requires a personal relationship with Christ. You accept Him as your personal Savior. All Christians have been adopted into His family. God's chosen people and Christ's church will go through the Great Tribulation.

God's chosen people, "the ones who believe in Christ," become a part of the church.

> There is neither Jew nor Greek, there is neither slave nor free, there is neither male nor female; for you are all one in Christ Jesus. And if you are Christ's, then you are Abraham's seed, and heirs according to the promise. (Gal. 3:28–29 NKJV)

We are the light of the world because of what lives within us. God's light shines through each Christian. Jesus is speaking: "You are the light of the world…" (Matt. 5:14a). In chapter 18 of Revelation, it speaks of the light and the bride: "The light of a lamp shall not shine in you anymore, and the voice of the bridegroom and bride shall not be heard anymore…" (Rev. 18:23 NKJV).

The bridegroom is Jesus, and the bride is a reference to the church. This is where God has already judged Babylon, the harlot, and after the bowls of the Great Tribulation.

What about the church at the end of time? Can the church be there with the Jews? From the beginning of time, God deals with man and man attempts to relate to God. God chose a people, and they became the Jewish nation. The Jewish nation needs to fellowship with God, and try to relate to Him, and be an example to a lost world. God's love has always been for everyone. His chosen people were the way for the world to see His love, to show His love, not try to regulate them. During Christ's physical life on earth, He reached out to the Jews first and then to the Gentiles. At the cross, Jesus made a way, and the church was born. The mission of the church is to share the good news of Jesus. With the cross and the good news of Jesus Christ, we are to share this message with the world. While the Jews were hung up on all of the rules and the laws, they wanted everyone to keep. The Gentiles started sharing love, and the church age came into being. The Jews did not go away. It will be the same when the 144,000 of the Jews are empowered: the Gentile believer will be there. Jew or Gentile, there is no other way to God except through Jesus Christ.

THE RAPTURE

Thomas had just asked a question: How can we know the way? "Jesus said to him, I am the way, the truth, and the life. No one comes to the Father except through Me" (John 14:6 NKJV).

In Mark chapter 13, it talks about the signs of end times, the coming of the Son of Man, the parable of the fig tree, and no one knows the hour or the day. Verses 1 and 2 is telling us about the destruction of the temple; then signs of the time, the things to look for; the Great Tribulation is coming (vv. 3–8). The Great Tribulation: persecution such as the world has never seen before or will ever see again (vv. 9–23). In verses 24–27, it is telling us that Christ will return. Verse 24 has a key to telling us when the rapture will take place: at the end of the Great Tribulation.

> But in those days, after the tribulation, the sun will be darkened, and the moon will not give its light; the stars of heaven will fall, and the powers in the heaven will be shaken. Then they will see the Son of Man coming in the clouds with great power and glory. And then He will send His angels, and gather together His elect from the four winds, from the farthest part of the earth to the farthest part of heaven. (Mark 13:24–27 NKJV)

Think about the characteristics of the Laodicea church age. They are lukewarm. I cannot think of anything to drink that I desire it lukewarm. We either want it hot or cold. You get water out of the tap. What do most people do? They put ice in it. Lukewarm is not good. The end-time church will be more concerned and consumed with taking care of the external aspect of the church building, and appearance. They have become more concerned about what they look like, their image, instead of the masses that need Jesus. Things should affect Christians, but we see gross sins every day, and it becomes no big deal. Christians hear so much over and over that it becomes acceptable. Sin in their minds becomes rationalized into an acceptable lifestyle. They say we (Christians) need to be more open and tolerant, but if we say they need to be more open and tolerant, those words become fighting words. They look at it as there right, not a decision to sin. People don't look at their lifestyle as sin, but it is their right to live as they see fit. Things that influence Christians are everyday events, and we become synthesized to the sin around us. We may not partake of the sin, but we do not stand in opposition to it either. Everyone rationalizes Satan's lies, and in our minds, it becomes okay (scary times for Christians). We know in our minds it is wrong, but we do nothing. In end time, our rights are more important than right and wrong. Christ will never rationalize sin into a personal right of ours. Sin is wrong, and God looks at sin for what it is: disobedience to Him. Satan's lies and deceptions are our undoing if we give him a foothold. We need to stay focused on Jesus Christ.

The rapture of the church will not happen before the Great Tribulation ends. The church will have to go through the Great Tribulation. Take heart, God will see us through this persecution. Our reward is in heaven. Never believe the lies Satan tells you. God loves each and every one of us! Amen! And Amen!

CHAPTER 12

John to Share

THE PURPOSE OF THE BOOK of Revelation is to reveal Jesus Christ as the Messiah. This was given to an angel and then to John.

The Scriptures are inspired. They are authoritative and without error in their original words and constitute the revelation of God to man. The Bible is God's word to man, not man's word about God. The Lord sent His angel to tell of things, which are to come. The angel's place is about the throne of God. Angel's relationship to believers is that of "ministering spirits." This is to the physical safety and well-being of the children of God. All the things that John saw, then wrote about, he added nothing to it of his own. All who believe in Christ as their Savior should read the Scripture. The Lord "will come quickly" and "is at hand" is never a positive affirmation that He will immediately appear. Only that He has the power to come at any time.

A local church is an assembly of professing believers in the Lord Jesus Christ. These believers mostly live in one locality and who meet together in His name for worship, praise, prayer, and fellowship. Baptism and the Lord's Supper are acts of obedience to the Lord. They are a testimony to show our walk with the Lord. The furtherance of the gospel is the announcement of a present God, the one who fulfills His covenant of the Spirit and the Lord. Wisdom, understanding, counsel, might, knowledge, and fear of the Lord show a true witness to God.

A follower of Christ doesn't lie; we follow His example. A false witness lies all the time to spread their untruth. Christ was the willing sacrifice for our sins. The blood of Christ is the only thing that can wash away our sins.

John gave this revelation to the world and this testimony of the things that he witnessed and shared with the church. They shared this so the church would not be unaware and not be caught sleeping. We are to read God's word and pray daily. Keep it in our hearts, and this is how we will not be caught sleeping. You will want to be in His presence if you love Him and be empowered by His love and grace. He will bestow blessings on your life every day when you live in His presence and power. Your relationship with Christ is every day, all day long, not once a week on Sunday morning—every day!

CHAPTER 13

Overview of Revelation

THE BOOK OF REVELATION TALKS about end times. It explains what is going to happen in the future, how far in the future no-one knows except God. It reveals the purpose of all the other books in the Bible. All the books lead to one point. They all point to the proclamation of Jesus Christ is the Savior of the world, the Messiah, and He will return one day for His church. Many people look at the book of Revelation as a book they want to avoid reading. There are so many unknowns. Things spoken of that will come to pass in our present day and in the future. Who would want to read about these things that are revealed? Something our culture feels is inappropriate and doesn't apply to us today.

Revelation is a book every Christian *must* read because it provides hope for the future. It talks about judgments that are coming. It affirms who we will be with for eternity when Christ arrives for the second time. Everybody should learn everything they can about the book of Revelation. Christians are to be ready and know what is happening around them and in the world. Revelation completes all the other books in the Bible and tells how things turn out.

IS THERE TIME

Interpreting the book of Revelation has been the topic of great discussion among men for centuries. There are several methods and views for interpreting Revelation:

There are four methods of interpreting Revelation:

First method of interpreting is exclusively to first-century events.
Second method of interpreting is the unfolding of church history until Christ's return.
Third method of interpreting is symbolizing eternal conflict between good and evil.
Fourth method of interpreting is about end times.

People blend some of these methods together when interpreting Revelation.

There are three different views of the millennium (a thousand years):

First view of the millennium: it sees no millennium and sees Christ as ruling spiritually in the church now.
Second view of the millennium: sees the spread of the gospel, and it will become more aggressively Christian. When the world becomes completely Christian, then there will be a millennium. That is when Christ will return.
Third view of the millennium: it sees Jesus return before the millennium and rules for a thousand years.

There are four views of the rapture (caught up):
This is the placement or timing of the church when it is raptured out of this world to be with Christ, as it relates to the Great Tribulation:

First view of rapture/pre-tribulation: this says the rapture will take place before the Great Tribulation starts.
Second view of rapture/mid-tribulation: this says the rapture will take place in the middle of the Great Tribulation.

OVERVIEW OF REVELATION

Third view of rapture/pre-wrath tribulation: this says the rapture will take place during the Great Tribulation, after the trumpets and before the wrath of God (the bowls).

Fourth view of rapture/post-tribulation: this says the rapture will take place at the end of the Great Tribulation, at Christ's return.

In the future, Christ will come back and remove the church. They will be with Christ forever from that point on. No matter what view you hold on the rapture, Christians are to watch and be ready for His return.

It is noteworthy to mention that the number three and seven are very important numbers in the Bible. God the Father, God the Son, and God the Holy Spirit make up the importance of the number three. God created the heavens and the earth and everything in them in seven days. The number seven means complete. Man will go through seven church ages. In each of the seals, trumpets, and bowls are seven parts of the warnings and judgments and wraths, three of seven. Christ will return, and Satan will be banished from the earth for a millennium.

I hope while you are waiting, you are watching, you are excited, and you desire and want the day to arrive. After the day arrives, Christ returns, and every Christian will be with the Lord forever.

We who Christ has saved because of our faith are part of the children of Abraham. Sons and coheirs to the promise that God made to Abraham.

> Understand, then, that those who believe are children of Abraham. The Scripture foresaw that God would justify the Gentiles by faith, and announced the gospel in advance to Abraham: All nations will be blessed through you. (Gal. 3:7–8 NIV)

What was the promise to Abraham that affects the people of God?

IS THERE TIME

> Now the Lord had said to Abram: 'Get out of your country, from your family and from your father's house, to a land that I will show you. I will make you a great nation; I will bless you and make your name great; and you shall be a blessing. I will bless those who bless you, and I will curse him who curses you; and in you all the families of the earth shall be blessed. (Gen. 12:1–3 NKJV)

God looked at Abram. "Then He brought Him outside and said, 'Look now toward heaven, and count the stars if you are able to number them.' And He said to him, 'So shall your descendants be. And he believed in the Lord, and He accounted it to him for righteousness'" (Gen. 15:5–6 NKJV).

Christ makes this promise relate to the Gentiles and to the Jews. The Gentiles, through faith in Christ, is part of this promise that God made to Abraham. After the cross, Jew or Gentile comes to the Father only through faith in Christ Jesus. Scripture tells us that there is God the Father, God the Son, and God the Holy Spirit, three in one.

> Jesus said to him, "I am the way, the truth, and the life. No one comes to the Father except through Me." (John 14:6 NKJV)

It didn't say "except the Jews." It says "no one comes to the Father except through Jesus." The only way after the cross to the Father is through Jesus. No great knowledge, birthright, special relationship to someone, only faith in Jesus Christ and a personal relationship with Christ are the ways to the Father.

The law was to show us our sin and our need for Christ.

> Therefore the law was our tutor to bring us to Christ, that we might be justified by faith. But

OVERVIEW OF REVELATION

after faith has come, we are no longer under a tutor. For you are all sons of God through faith in Christ Jesus. For as many of you as we're baptized into Christ have put on Christ. There is neither Jew nor Greek, there is neither slave nor free, there is neither male nor female; for you are all one in Christ Jesus. And if you are Christ's, then you are Abraham's seed, and heirs according to the promise. (Gal. 3:24–29 NKJV)

There are three major parts to the book of Revelation:

- First, there is the proclamation: Jesus Christ is the Son of God, the Messiah.
- Second, the church age: it explains what is to happen between the cross and the return of Christ.
- Third, the description of the end of the ages and a new heaven and earth: it tells what humanity is to expect as the end approaches and comes to the final state man will be.

There are seven divisions in the book of Revelation:

Introduction	chapter 1
Church Age	chapter 2–3

1: the church of Ephesus
2: the church of Smyrna
3: the church of Pergamos
4: the church of Thyatira
5: the church of Sardis
6: the church of Philadelphia
7: the church of Laodicea

The throne room, seven seals, seven trumpets, seven bowls	chapter 4–16

The beast of the sea/the beast of the earth
Fall of Babylon   chapter 17–18
Christ's return and a one-thousand-year reign   chapter 19
Satan crushed and the judgment   chapter 20
Names not in the Book of Life
New heaven and new earth   chapter 21–22

We need to have a basic understanding of the concepts that help us as we read through the book of Revelation, and these next three steps are very important to gain understanding.

Pray that God will show you what He wants you to understand as you read and meditate on His word.

Take the time to listen! Don't be in such a hurry. You may skip over what the Lord wants for you. Let the word become a part of your life.

Realize that no one has all the answers but God.

I hope that reading this overview will inspire you to pick up the Bible and read it, study it, and absorber it. Dig into the Scripture as God leads you and watch Him bless. God leading you is an important part of your study of His word. Always read God's word with an open mind and heart. No matter how many times you have read and studied the Bible, God will show you something new. Just because you learned something great several years ago doesn't mean He is through showing you new and wonderful things, but we need to read it and let Him lead you. I had a teacher several years ago. He was a man that was very smart and knew a lot of technical things in the Bible. He could tell you facts and get them all right. But in class, he was teaching and sharing the great message God gave him ten years ago and didn't change or add any new relevant revelations. The Bible is the living word of God. It reveals new and exciting inspiration to us. The Word applies to us no matter where we are in our walk with the Lord.

OVERVIEW OF REVELATION

Ask God to enter and fill your mind and heart with His love, guidance, and wisdom. Always seek his will and guidance when reading His Word. It makes all the difference in your understanding of what you are reading. One of the most important things you can remember is *His will, not yours.*

Revelation 1

Revelation reveals Jesus Christ to the world, and that He is the Messiah. The church is the bride of Christ. It talks about the greeting to the seven churches. Christ loves us and washes away our sins with His blood. He will return, and we will meet Him in the clouds one day and every person: man, woman, and child will see this event. When John saw this vision, he and the believers were suffering persecution. Paul said that there would be many trials and persecution during the tribulation periods. Believers have to overcome these persecutions until the return of Christ. He will "strengthen the souls of the disciples, exhorting them to continue in the faith, and saying, 'We must through many tribulations enter the kingdom of God'" (Acts 14:22 NKJV).

The Trinity is God the Father, God the Son, and God the Holy Spirit—three in one. All three have existed from the beginning, now, and in the future. God has always been and will always be. "Grace" was a Christian greeting common from the Greeks, and "Peace" was a common greeting from the Hebrews.

> John, to the seven churches which are in Asia:
> Grace to you and peace from Him who is and
> who was and who is to come. (Rev. 1:4a NKJV)

Christ is the rightful ruler, but will not exert His authority until He returns for the second time. The first time Christ came, he came to serve and to save all that would listen to his message. But when he returns, He will come in power and glory and His presence will radiate to all that come in contact with Him and hear Him.

> And from Jesus Christ, the faithful witness, the firstborn from the dead, and the ruler over the kings of the earth. To Him who loved us and washed us from our sins in His own blood. (Rev. 1:5 NKJV)

Paul was speaking to the elders of the church. There were elders appointed in every church. When Christ comes to earth for the second time, He will come in the clouds, and every eye will see Him. Christ is the Alpha and the Omega, the beginning and the end.

> I was in the Spirit on the Lord's Day, and I heard behind me a loud voice, as a trumpet, saying, "I am there Alpha and the Omega, the First and the Last, and, What you see, write in a book and send it to the seven churches which are in Asia: to Ephesus, to Smyrna, to Pergamos, to Thyatira, to Sardis, to Philadelphia, to Laodicea." (Rev. 1:10–11 NKJV)

The seven churches are the light of the world. We are to let the light of Jesus shine out of us. The light of Jesus is what people are to see. They are to see Jesus, not us. We walk and are the light in a dark world, so we are to put our light where Jesus leads us. Let the light that is within you shine.

> The seven stars are the angels of the seven churches, and the seven lamp stands which you saw are the seven churches. (Rev. 1:20 NKJV)

Revelation 2 and 3

The letters to seven churches, represent the different ages the church will go through. Jesus had several things to say about all seven of the churches. The letters covers the four basic aspects that concerned Jesus: I know, instruction, criticism, and promise. The letters to the churches in chapter 2 and 3 are covered in the chapter "The Church Age."

Revelation 4 and 5

Chapter 4 starts the account of the second vision of John. These are important chapters in the book of Revelation because the book changes at this point. Before chapter 4, the book covers the revelation of Jesus Christ as the Messiah, the church age, and how it pertains to end times. Starting with chapter 4 and going through chapter 20, it starts to focus on occurrences in the future and the apocalypse.

In Revelation 4:1, the phrase "Come up here" has captured people's attention as long as people have been reading this book.

> After these things I looked, and behold, a door standing open in heaven. And the first voice which I heard was like a trumpet speaking with me, saying, "Come up here, and I will show you things which must take place after this." (Rev. 4:1 NKJV)

Some consider this a command to the church, the rapture of the church before the great tribulation. Some consider this a style of writing to introduce John's vision. John was taken in the spirit to heaven to see the things to come. "Immediately I was in the Spirit; and behold, a throne set in heaven, and One sat on the throne" (Rev. 4:2 NKJV). When it says, "Immediately I was in the Spirit," John is the one talking here, and he was the one in the Spirit, not the church.

The twenty-four elders fall down and worship the one on the throne and cast their crowns before Him. These twenty-four elders may relate to the twelve tribes of the children of Israel and the twelve apostles of Christ (the chosen and the faithful). These elders function as ruling priest in the present age.

> Around the throne were twenty-four thrones, and on the thrones I saw twenty-four elders sit-

ting, clothed in white robes; and they had crowns of gold on their heads. And from the throne proceeding lightings, thunderings, and voices. Seven lamps of fire were burning before the throne, which are the seven Spirits of God. (Rev. 4:4–5 NKJV)

The white robes indicate righteousness. The crowns show the elders possessing ruling authority. At the end of each of the seals, trumpets, and bowls are the warnings. There is lighting and thunder.

God has always dealt with people individually, even when He was dealing with His chosen people. He would use specific individuals to bring His people back to Him. When we, the Gentile believer, accept Christ as our personal Savior, we partake of the promise to Abraham. The seven lamps are the Spirits of God. The angels of the seven churches are spirit beings who minister to believers.

In the Old Testament, it was God's chosen people giving sacrifice to God to make atonement to God. In the New Testament, it is believing in Jesus Christ. He is the one that can cross the span that our sins separates us from God. God always provides a way to Himself, no matter how man keeps reinforcing the separation from God, our sin.

Old Testament		New Testament	
People—Israel—to—Sacrifice—to—God		People—Believers—to—Jesus Christ—to—God	
The Time of the Jew		The Time of the Gentile	
Jews—God's Chosen People—Saints		Church—Bride of Christ—Saints	
Deuteronomy 33:2	Angelic beings	Acts 26:10	People—Believers/Individual
1 Samuel 2:9	People—Israel/Nation	Romans 1:7	People—Believers/Individual

OVERVIEW OF REVELATION

2 Chronicles 6:14	People—Israel/Nation	8:27	People—Believers/Individual
Psalms 16:3	People—Israel/Nation	16:2	People—Believers/Individual
30:4	People—Israel/Nation	1 Corinthians 1:2	People—Believers/Individual
31:21	People—Israel/Nation	6:2	People—Believers/Individual
34:9	People—Israel/Nation	Ephesians 1:15	People—Believers/Individual
37:28	People—Israel/Nation	1:18	People—Believers/Individual
50:5	People—Israel/Nation	2:19	People—Believers/Individual
97:10	People—Israel/Nation	3:8	People—Believers/Individual
116:15	People—Israel/Nation	4:12	People—Believers/Individual
145:10	People—Israel/Nation	6:18	People—Believers/Individual
148:14	People—Israel/Nation	Colossians 1:12	People—Believers/Individual
149:1	People—Israel/Nation	1 Thessalonians 3:13	People—Believers/Individual
149:5	People—Israel/Nation	2 Thessalonians 1:10	People—Believers/Individual
Proverbs 2:8	People—Israel/Nation	1 Timothy 5:10	People—Believers/Individual
Daniel: 7:18	End Times—People—Individual	Philemon 1:7	People—Believers/Individual
7:21	End Times—People—Individual	Jude 3	People—Believers/Individual
7:25	End Times—People—Individual	Revelation 5:8	People—Believers/Individual
7:27	End Times—People—Individual	15:3	People—Believers/Individual
		16:6	People—Believers/Individual

IS THERE TIME

In the Old Testament, "Saints" are referred to as angelic beings or God's people from Abraham to Christ.

In the New Testament, "Saints" are referred to as the church, the bride of Christ.

> To the church of God which is at Corinth, to those who are sanctified in Christ Jesus, called to be saints, with all who in every place call on the name of Jesus Christ our Lord, both theirs and ours: Grace to you and peace from God our Father and the Lord Jesus Christ. (1 Cor. 1:2–3 NKJV)

Where it says saints, these are the believers in Christ, His church. The New Testament did not replace the Old Testament; it fulfills the Old Testament. God has always related to individual people from the beginning of time. He relates to individuals and to nations. After the cross, it is an individual relating through Christ. He still has a chosen people. He will always watch over the nation of Israel. There is a new element mixed in with the old in man's relationship with the Father. That element is Christ. After the cross, no matter who you are, Jew or Gentile, they must go through Christ to reach the Father.

> Jesus said to him, "I am the way, the truth, and the life. No one comes to the Father except through Me." (John 14:6 NKJV)

John is now in heaven and sees the four living creatures giving glory, praise, honor, and thanks to the one who sits on the throne.

> The first living creature was like a lion, the second living creature like a calf, the third living creature had a face like a man, and the fourth living creature was like a flying eagle. (Rev. 4:7 NKJV)

OVERVIEW OF REVELATION

First, the living creature is a lion. This is a reference to the Gospel of Matthew and was written for the Jews. Second, the living creature is a calf. This is a reference to the Gospel of Mark and was written for the Romans. Third, a living creature has a face like a man. This is a reference to the Gospel of Luke and was written for the Greeks. Fourth, the living creature is a flying eagle. This is a reference to the Gospel of John and was written for everyone.

> And I heard, as it were, the voice of a great multitude, as the sound of many waters and as the sound mighty thunderings, saying, "Alleluia! For the Lord God Omnipotent reigns! Let us be glade and rejoice and give Him glory, for the marriage of the Lamb has come, and His wife has made herself ready." And to her it was granted to be arrayed in fine linen, clean and bright, for the fine linen is the righteous acts of the saints. (Rev. 19:6–8 NKJV)

The saints are the bride of Christ. "The marriage of the Lamb" is the consummation of the marriage of Christ to His church. Marriage of His bride has three stages: the betrothal, bride, and rapture. Betrothal is when people accept Christ as their personal Savior, and they become members of the body of Christ. Bride is the church, and the bridegroom is Christ, and He will come for the bride. Rapture is when the bride, the church (saints) is caught up to the sky to meet Christ in the air.

> The four living creatures, each having six wings, were full of eyes around and within. And they do not rest day or night, saying: "Holy, holy, holy Lord God Almighty, who was and is and is to come!" (Rev. 4:8 NKJV)

The four living creatures don't stop day or night; they praise God. They give glory, honor, and thanks to God, who lives forever and ever. The twenty-four elders fall down and worship Him who lives forever and cast their crowns before the throne, saying, "You are worthy, O Lord, to receive glory and honor and power; for you created all things, and by Your will they exist and were created" (Rev. 4:11 NKJV).

John wept, because they could not find no one who was worthy to read the scroll, or even look at it.

> But one of the elders said to me, "Do not weep. Behold, the Lion of the tribe of Judah, the Root of David, has prevailed to open the scroll and to loose its seven seals." (Rev. 5:5 NKJV)

The Lamb takes the scroll out of the right hand of the one who sat on the throne. Now the four living creatures and the twenty-four elders fall down before the Lamb and sing a new song:

> And they sing a new song: "You are worthy to take the scroll, and to open its seals; for You were slain, and have redeemed us to God by Your blood out of ever tribe and tongue and people and nation, and have made us kings and priest to our God; and we shall reign on the earth." (Rev. 5:9–10 NKJV)

Then the voice of the angels joined the four living creatures and the twenty-four elders.

> And the number of them was ten thousand times ten thousand, and thousand of thousands, saying with a loud voice: "Worthy is the Lamb who was slain to receive power and riches and wisdom, and strength and honor and glory and blessing!" (Rev. 5:11b–12 NKJV)

Then every creature in heaven and earth, John heard, saying, "Blessing and honor and glory and power be to Him, who sits on the throne, and to the Lamb, forever and ever!" (Rev. 5:13b NKJV). "Then the four living creatures said, 'Amen!' And the twenty-four elders fell down and worshiped Him who lives forever and ever" (Rev. 5:14 NKJV).

Every living thing in heaven sings this new song, and the praise is to God the Father and the Son. All are in awe and reverence to the King, the creator of everything that exists in heaven, earth, and any place in-between.

Revelation 6

The First Seal: The conqueror is the Antichrist coming to deceive the world that he is the returning messiah. Reference to Revelation 6:1–2.

The Second Seal: The earth is in conflict and there is no peace. People will rise and kill one another, as the world has never seen before. Reference to Revelation 6:3–4.

The Third Seal: There will be the worst famine ever on this earth. Reference to Revelation 6:5–6.

The Fourth Seal: There will be widespread death on earth. The second and the third seals are things that Israel has seen before when God brought them back to repentance. It's a wake-up call for the inhabitants of the earth. Reference to Revelation 6:7–8.

The Fifth Seal: The cry of the martyrs goes up to God. The slain Saints that stand on the word of God cry out how long, Lord, avenge our blood. Reference to Revelation 6:9–11.

The Sixth Seal: The earth changes: earthquakes, the sun turns black, and the moon becomes red as blood. The stars fall; every mountain and island has moved from its place. Every man runs and tries to find a hiding place from all the disturbances of nature. Reference to Revelation 6:12–17.

In the last part of the sixth seal, it says, "Every slave and every free man." Every slave is a reference to men in sin, and every free man is a reference to men made free in Christ, the church. We need to look at the last two letters to see what promises Jesus made to them. There are seven letters to the churches and the last two are Philadelphia and Laodicean.

A blessing promise to Philadelphia, which is the second to last church age, a promise because of their faithfulness. They were a church in revival. This age was overcoming what the world was throwing at them. The believers of this church age were staying true to God's principles. Christ will keep them from the hour of trial, which will come on the earth. Believers of this church age, Philadelphia, will be protected from what is coming. The Laodicean age had no blessing promise because they are lukewarm. He will vomit them out of His mouth. This is the last church age. There is a huge difference between the two church ages. Around the time Israel became a nation, the church was transitioning from the Philadelphia church age to the Laodicea church age. The Philadelphia church age: "Because you have kept My command to persevere, I also will keep you from the hour of trial which shall come upon the whole world, to test those who dwell on the earth" (Rev. 3:10 NKJV).

During the last part of the Laodicea church age, the 144,000 Jews and the Great Tribulation will happen. We need to keep in mind that somewhere on this planet, there has always been some kind of persecution going on. The End-Time Tribulation will continue to be until the end of the seals and the beginning of the trumpets. Persecution differs from place to place, and as the time draws near, the persecution will get worse and more widespread. Around the world, some governments protect and some persecute. It depends on self-centeredness related to believing in a higher being. People don't worry about what God thinks of the sin they commit, because sin has been rationalized to be okay. Our sinful nature has a hard time letting us believe that someone other than ourselves is in control of our lives, our destiny.

The Laodicea church age has a different promise: "So then, because you are lukewarm, and neither cold nor hot, I will vomit you out of My mouth" (Rev. 3:16 NKJV). That's not what I would call a great promise. The believer will have to prove what they believe. Our words will not be enough; it will require action and sacrifice. The

Christians will be tested. At this time, will we stand for Jesus Christ and be persecuted or stand with the world that rationalizes sin to be okay. The people of this age will not be ashamed of showing their bodies off with little or next to nothing on. For men and women to show the features of their body, that at one time in the not too distant past, would be unthinkable and now think nothing of it. People in this age, wealth is thought to bring happiness and a sign of success. Everything in this age revolves around wealth. The more money you have, the greater and more successful you are. Their world tries to convince us true happiness can only be from worldly wealth, money.

> Because you say, "I am rich, have become wealthy, and have need of nothing"—and do not know that you are wretched, miserable, poor, blind, and naked—I counsel you to buy from Me gold refined in the fire, that you may be rich; and white garments, that you may be clothed, that the shame of your nakedness may not be revealed; and anoint your eyes with eye salve, that you may see. As many as I love, I rebuke and chasten. Therefore be zealous and repent. (Rev. 3:17–19 NKJV)

The church, people of the Laodicea age, will go through the time of the Great Tribulation. They will be tested for their faith and for how they follow God's word. The people of this time will be concerned about their image more than about their relationship with Christ. Satan has deceived the people of the Laodicea age. He has blinded them from seeing the truth. They will think they are doing what God wants. Instead of accomplishing great things for God, they will spin their wheels, accomplishing nothing. Their accomplishments will appear to be what God wants. They are neither hot nor cold. What a terrible state of mind for the church to be in. Now that is scary.

God has a chosen people, the Jews. He tried to work through the Jews up to the cross. God tried to have fellowship with the Jews.

He desires to have fellowship with His creation. He required one thing from His chosen people: to be faithful to Him. The Jewish nation had a problem remaining faithful from one generation to the next.

After the cross, the church age started. There is a description of each church at the beginning of the book of Revelation in chapter 2 and 3. It shows how each will behave. Church age relates differently than when the Jews related to God. Church age is the time of the Gentile. The Jews will gain some authority in the Great Tribulation when the 144,000 from the tribes of Israel take their place, as it is talked about in chapter 7. It comes down to they have to understand the Trinity: God the Father, God the Son, and God the Holy Spirit. All three are one. From the time of the cross, both Jew and Gentile, all must come through Jesus to reach God. Christ is the Messiah! No one goes to the Father except through Christ.

Revelation 7

John had another vision. There are two visions in this chapter: sealing the 144,000 of the tribes of Israel and a great multitude that no one could number from the Great Tribulation.

There are four angels standing in all four corners of the earth. They were ready to hold the four winds from blowing on the earth, seas, and trees. An angel from heaven is carrying the seal of the living God. The four angels with a loud voice were granted to harm the earth, sea, and trees until the servants of our God have been sealed. The amount of the servants sealed numbered 144,000. They will be 12,000 from each of the twelve tribes of Israel. The twelve tribes of Israel are Judah, Reuben, Gad, Asher, Naphtali, Manasseh, Simeon, Levi, Issachar, Zebulun, Joseph, and Benjamin. All twelve tribes of the children of Israel, 12,000, form each tribe, equal 144,000 sealed.

There was a multitude of people from all nations, tribes, and tongues clothed in white robes standing before the throne of God and before the Lamb. With a loud voice saying, "Salvation belongs to our God who sits on the throne, and the Lamb!" All the angels standing around the throne fell down and worshiped God before the living creatures and the elders, saying, "Amen! Blessing, glory, wisdom, thanksgiving, honor, power and might, be to our God forever and ever, Amen." Reference to Revelation 7:10–12.

This great multitude, the robes washed white with the blood of the Lamb. These are the ones coming out of the Great Tribulation, and there are large numbers of Christians. The believers stand up for Christ and don't hide. They profess with boldness that Jesus Christ is Lord. They will give their lives for the cause of Christ. This martyrdom lets the world know where these Christians stand with their relationship to Christ. They are no longer hungry or thirsty anymore. The Lamb will shepherd and lead them to the living fountains of water.

God seals the 144,000 Jews to prepare them for the tribulation to come. He also tells us of the ones that are coming out of the Great Tribulation to encourage us in our faith and that there is a reward coming to those who endure to the end. The rewards are great. The losses are devastating. The choices we make today will determine where we spend eternity: heaven or hell—and they are both very real places.

Revelation 8

John returns to the second vision and picks up with the opening of the seventh seal. The seventh seal is the final seal opened before the trumpets.

The Seventh Seal: When the seal is opened, there is silence in heaven. There are seven angels before God, and trumpets were given to them. Another angel came before the altar carrying a golden censer. They offered incense and all the prayers of the saints upon the golden altar, before the throne. The smoke of the incense and the prayers of the saints rose to God. The angel took the golden censer, filled it with fire from the altar, and threw it to the earth: "And there were noises, thundering, lightings, and earthquakes." Reference to Revelation 8:1–7.

Then the angels that had the seven trumpets prepared to sound them. Trumpets were used in the past to gather the Lord's people, to assemble the Lord's army, to prepare for battle, and to announce a new king. The sounding of the seven trumpets is a declaration of war.

The First Trumpet Sounds: Hail and fire mingled with blood cast down to earth. A third of all the trees and all the grasses burned up. Reference to Revelation 8:7.
The Second Trumpet Sounds: A great mountain burning with fire is cast into the sea. There was a third of the seas became blood. A third of the sea creatures died. Out of all the ships, a third of them destroyed. Reference to Revelation 8:8–9.
The Third Trumpet Sounds: A star fell from heaven burning like a torch, and the star fell on a third of the rivers and springs of water. The name of the star is Wormwood. A third of the waters became Wormwood, and men died. The water was bitter. Reference to Revelation 8:10–11.
The Fourth Trumpet Sounds: A third of the sun, moon, and the stars became dark. A third of the day and the night didn't shine. An angel with a loud voice in heaven said, "Woe, woe, woe" to the inhabitants of the earth, because the remaining blasts of the trumpets are about to sound. Reference to Revelation 8:12–13.

First four trumpets are directed at the creation of God. The next three are directed at the inhabitants of the earth, the humans. First four trumpets will happen in a very short time from each other. It's interesting to note that the angel announced woe three times, and there are three trumpets left to blow.

God warns the inhabitants of the earth repeatedly, "Repent. I am coming one day." He tells us in nature. He tells us in His word to open your eyes and see, open your ears and hear. In each letter addressed to the seven churches, it says, "He who has an ear, let him hear what the Spirit says to the church."

OVERVIEW OF REVELATION

Revelation 9

The Fifth Trumpet Sounds: There was a star (an angel) falling from heaven to earth, and he had the key to the bottomless pit. When he opened the pit, smoke came out and darkened the sun and the air. Out of the smoke came locus, and they have power like scorpions. The locusts have instruction not to harm the grass or the trees. The locusts could not harm men that had the seal from God on their foreheads. Their power was to hurt men for five months. *The first woe is passed*, and there are two more woes to come. The second woe is worse than the first, and the third woe is worse than the other two put together. Reference to Revelation 9:1–12.

The Sixth Trumpet Sounds: The angel sounds the sixth trumpet. One who had the sixth trumpet said, "Release the four angels bound at the Euphrates River." The four angels are released. The heads of the houses they ride are like lions; and out of their mouth come fire, smoke, and brimstone. From these three plagues, a third of humanity dies. Their power came from their mouth and their tails. Their tails are like a serpent's head, and they do harm. Reference to Revelation 9:13–21.

Humanity did not repent after seeing these killed. They should not have worshiped demons, idols of gold, silver, brass, and wood. They did not repent of being murders, sorcerers, sexually immoral, and thievery.

Revelation 10

This is another vision John saw. A mighty angel came from heaven clothed with a cloud, a rainbow on his face. His face was like the sun; his feet were like pillars of fire. He had a little book in his hand. His right foot was in the sea, and his left foot was on land. With a loud voice like a lion, he cried out the Seven Thunders Uttered. Then a voice from heaven said, "Seal up the things that the Seven Thunders Uttered." The angel standing on the sea and on the land raised his hands to heaven. He swore by Him who lives forever and ever who created heaven, earth, seas, and the things in them. There should be no more delay. In the sounding of the seventh angel, the mystery of God would be finished.

John was told to go and eat from the little book. He approached the angel and asks for the book and ate from the book. It was sweet as honey in his mouth. After he had eaten from the book, his stomach became bitter. The angel told John, "You must prophesy about this book to the people, nations, and kings." When people read this book, this prophesy will seem sweet because of the victory. But when people thoroughly read the book, it becomes bitter because of the judgments coming. We are to continue to share this message with the world.

Revelation 11

John returns to the second vision and picks up with the two witnesses. The Gentiles will inhabit the outside court of the temple and tread the city under foot for forty-two months. The two witnesses will be given power during this time. They will prophesy for 1,260 days. "So he said, 'These are the two anointed ones, who stand beside the Lord of the whole earth'" (Zech. 4:14 NKJV). The angel is talking just before this verse to Zechariah. If anyone attempts to harm the two witnesses, fire from their mouth will devour them. The two will stop the water of heaven from falling. The earth's water will turn to blood. Many plagues come as often as the two desires.

When the two witnesses have finished their testimony, the beast that ascended out of the bottomless pit makes war on them. The beast overcomes the two witnesses and kills them. Their dead bodies will lie in the street for three and a half days. The location is the same place that they crucified our Lord. All the people of the earth, no matter what nation they are from, will see the two lying in the street. They will not bury them. Everyone on the earth rejoiced and was in great happiness because the two that tormented the ones on the earth are dead.

OVERVIEW OF REVELATION

After three and a half days, God breathed life back into the two witnesses. They stood up. The ones who saw God breathe life back into them were in great fear. Then a loud voice from heaven said to the two witnesses, "Come up here." They ascended to heaven, and their enemies saw them ascend. In the same hour, there was a great earthquake and a tenth of the city fell. There were seven thousand killed in the earthquake. The rest of the people were afraid, so they gave glory to God. *The second woe has passed*, and the third woe is coming.

The Seventh Trumpet Sounds: The seventh trumpet sounded, before the bowls of God's wrath are poured out on the world. "And the twenty-four elders who sat before God on their thrones fell on their faces and worshiped God, saying: 'We give You thanks, O Lord God Almighty, the One who is and who was and who is to come, because You have taken Your great power and reigned. The nations were angry, and Your wrath has come, and the time of the dead, that they should be judged, and that You should reward Your servants the prophets and the saints, and those who fear Your name, small and great, and should destroy those who destroy the earth.'" Reference to Revelation 11:16–18.

John could see into the temple, and he saw the ark of the covenant. Then he heard lightning, noises, thunder, earthquake, and great hail.

Revelation 12

John has another vision before the bowls of God's wrath.

> Now a great sign appeared in heaven: a woman clothed with the sun, with the moon under her feet, and on her head a garland of twelve stars. (Rev. 12:1 NKJV)

IS THERE TIME

Satan attempts to prevent the increase of the church. "Clothed with the sun," as Christ came out of the nation of Israel and began His ministry. After He was gone from earth, the apostles shared about Christ to all the people, Jews and Gentiles. People began accepting Christ as their personal Savior. The moon under her feet could be the earth beneath the people. Her heart and hope are on the things in heaven. There are three realms referred to as heaven in the Bible: the earth and its atmosphere, the sun and moon and stars, and then the dwelling place of God. The garland of twelve stars could be the twelve tribes of Israel or the doctrine of the gospel preached by the twelve apostles. Many things relate the Old Testament and the New Testament together. They tie the things of the past to the things of the future. The woman was with child. She cried out in pain and gave birth to the child. This child could be Christ. This struggle between Satan and woman is nothing new. In Genesis 3:15, Satan tempted woman in the garden.

> And another sign appeared in heaven: behold, a great, fiery red dragon having seven heads and ten horns, and seven diadems on his heads. His tail drew a third of the starts of heaven and threw them to the earth. And the dragon stood before the woman who was ready to give birth, to devour the Child as soon as it was born. She bore a male Child who was to rule all nations with a rod of iron. And her Child was caught up to God and His throne. (Rev. 12:3–5 NKJV)

The fiery red dragon is Satan. Satan appeared first in the Bible back in the garden of Edom as the Serpent. The seven heads and ten horns could refer to the empire over which Satan rules during the time when he is not in heaven and abides on earth. The seven heads, ten horns, and diadems could refer to Satan's power and glory as "god of this age." Daniel refers to the seven heads and ten horns in chapter 7 and 8 of the book of Daniel.

OVERVIEW OF REVELATION

"His tail drew a third of the stars from heaven and threw them to earth…." This referred to a third of the angels that rebelled with Satan. "And the Dragon stood before the woman who was ready to give birth, to devour her child as soon as it was born." The dragon stood before the woman to devour her child could be a reference to when Herod attempts to kill the newborn child, Christ. "She bore a male Child who was to rule all nations with rod of iron. And her Child was caught up to God and His throne" (Rev. 12:4–5 NKJV).

The Child taken to God and His throne, this child is Jesus. The caught up is reference to the ascension of Christ. A place of protection for the woman in the wilderness could be a reference to an example of what had happened for Israel in the Sinai wilderness in Exodus 16. The 1,260 days are the provision and protection for the woman in the wilderness, the Jewish nation. Some think that this is reference to half of the seven-year tribulation period. In the seventy weeks of Daniel, there are sixty-two weeks, seven weeks, and one week. This makes up the seventy weeks. The one week is a seven-year period. Three and a half years of Christ ministry and three and a half years of Satan's rule at the end.

War broke out in heaven. Michael and his angels fought with the dragon and his angels. The dragon did not win, and there was no place for the dragon and his angels in heaven anymore. Dragon (the one called the serpent, devil, Satan), the deceiver of the world, and his angels were cast down to earth. The one who accused the brethren before God day and night is no longer in heaven and has no access. This is *the third woe*.

> Therefore rejoice, O heavens, and you who dwell in them! Woe to the inhabitants of the earth and the sea! For the devil has come down to you, having great wrath, because he knows that he has short time. (Rev. 12:12 NKJV)

This means that Satan cannot enter heaven, and he is confined to earth. Everyone in heaven has good reason to rejoice when Satan is bound to earth. Satan knows his time is short, and he is to abide in the bottomless pit. Satan's anger grows, and he will unleash his wrath on the remaining inhabitants.

The woman who gave birth to the male child is Israel. The male child is Christ, and the woman encompasses the church. Israel will be given wings to fly to a safe place that is provided. At the safe place, she can be nourished for a time and time and a half. A time and times and a half could mean forty-two months or three-and-a-half years.

> And the dragon was enraged with the woman, and he went to make war with the rest of her offspring, who keep the commandments of God and have the testimony of Jesus Christ. (Rev. 12:17 NKJV)

God protects Israel. They were no longer in the serpent's presence. There was spewed water as if a flood on earth came from the serpent. The earth opened up and took the water and helped the Israelites. The dragon was furious that he could not get to the Israelites. When he couldn't get to the Israelites, he turned on the rest of the believers in Christ, the church (saints).

With the nation of Israel in a safe place, Jewish and Gentile believers are the church, and now Satan makes war. He will oppose anything with a trace of Christ showing in their life. Who keeps the commandments of God is the Jewish nation. The testimony of Jesus Christ is the church.

Revelation 13

The thirteenth chapter of Revelation has a direct correlation to the dream of Nebuchadnezzar in Daniel 2:31–45. The dream that Nebuchadnezzar had was that a man standing in armor, head protected with gold, chest and arms with silver, belly and thighs with bronze, legs with iron, and feet with iron and clay. The Babylon Empire was in power at the time of Nebuchadnezzar's dream. These are the world empires that will rise to power and then pass.

OVERVIEW OF REVELATION

the head	gold	the Babylon Empire
the chest and arms	silver	the Med-Persia Empire
the belly and thighs	bronze	the Greece Empire
the legs	iron	the Roman Empire
the feet	iron and clay	the restored Roman Empire

> You, O king, were watching; and behold, a great image! This great image, whose splendor was excellent, stood before you, and its form was awesome. This image's head was of fine gold, its chest and arms of silver, its belly and thighs of bronze, its legs of iron, its feet partly of iron and partly of clay. (Dan. 2:31–33 NKJV)

The last one has two elements, iron and clay, two ruling powers. This represents two feet, the beast from the sea and land in Revelation 13. The restored Roman Empire represents a political and religious power. Two feet have ten toes refer to ten horns and ten crowns. All five empires pass and are no more.

> Then the iron, the clay, the bronze, the silver, and the gold were crushed together, and became like chaff from the summer threshing floors; the wind carries them away so that no trace of them was found. And the stone that struck the image became a great mountain and filled the whole earth. (Dan. 2:35 NKJV)

The stone that strikes will be one who breaks these empires and will stand forever.

> Inasmuch as you saw that the stone was cut out of the mountain without hands, and that it broke in pieces the iron, the bronze, the clay, the silver, and the gold-the great God has made known to

> the king what will come to pass after this. The dream is certain, and its interpretation is sure. (Dan. 2:45 NKJV)

Jesus Christ is the cornerstone.

The beast of the sea has seven heads, ten horns, and ten crowns and on his heads a blasphemous name. The seven heads could be Assyria, Babylon, Egypt, Greece, Persia, Rome, and a restored Roman Empire. The ten horns could be the Gentile world power as it relates to Israel. The beast that John saw was like a leopard, feet like a bear, and a mouth like a lion.

> Then I stood on the sand of the sea. And I saw a beast rising up out of the sea, having seven heads and ten horns, and on the horns ten crowns, and on his heads a blasphemous name. Now the beast which I saw was like a leopard, his feet were like the feet of a bear, and his mouth of a lion. The dragon gave him his power, his throne, and great authority. (Rev. 13:1–2 NKJV)

Now compare Daniel 7:2–8 to what you just read in Revelation 13:1–2.

Daniel spoke, "The first was like a lion and had eagle's wings (Dan. 7:4a NKJV), a second like a bear (Dan. 5:5b NKJV), a third like a leopard (Dan. 7:6b NKJV), and a fourth like a beast (Dan. 7:7a NKJV). And there, in this horn, were eyes like the eyes of a man and a mouth speaking pompous words (Dan. 7:2–8 NKJV)."

The lion represents king or ruler of the land, and the eagle represents king or ruler of the air. In Daniel's vision of the four beasts, it looks a lot like the beast of the sea in Revelation.

OVERVIEW OF REVELATION

Daniel 7:3	Revelation 13:1
"And four beast came up from the sea…"	"Saw a beast rising up out of the sea…"
Daniel 7:2	Revelation 7:1
"The four winds of heaven were stirring…up the Great sea"	"The four corners of earth holding four winds of the earth…"
Daniel 7:4	Revelation 13:2
"The first was like a lion…"	"His mouth like the mouth of a lion…"
Daniel 7:5	Revelation 13:2
"A second, like a bear…"	"His feet were like the feet of a bear…"
Daniel 7:6	Revelation 13:2
"Another, like a leopard…"	"Now the beast which I saw was like a leopard…"
Daniel 7:7	Revelation 13:1
"A fourth beast…it was different… It had ten horns."	"Having seven heads and ten horns…"
Daniel 7:8	Revelation 13:1
"Speaking pompous words"	"On his heads a blasphemous name"

The dragon gave the beast his power, his throne, and great authority. This beast was mortally wounded, and his wound healed. The world marveled at the one who had a deadly wound and came back from it. They worshiped the dragon, who gave authority to the beast. The world worships the beast, and they have been convinced that he is a power that no one can match. If they worship the beast, they are worshiping the Satan. The people said, "Who is like the beast? Who can make war with him?"

The beast speaking blasphemies against God, and the ones in heaven have authority to continue for forty-two months. He will make war on all who believe in Christ. The beast will overcome the saints. Anyone's name not found in the Book of Life will worship the beast. "If anyone has an ear, let him hear" (Rev. 13:9 NKJV).

IS THERE TIME

In chapter 2 and 3 of Revelation, all have the same quote about the different church ages.

Revelation 2:7—Ephesus
Revelation 2:11—Smyrna
Revelation 2:17—Pergamos
Revelation 2:29—Thyatira
Revelation 3:6—Sardis
Revelation: 3:13—Philadelphia
Revelation 3:22—Laodicea

"He who has an ear, let him hear what the Spirit says to the churches."
There will be persecution and martyrdom for all believers in Christ during the Great Tribulation. Believers will face being tortured, imprisoned, and even killed for their faith. They are to have patience and faith. They know the Lord will vindicate them on the day of wrath and righteous judgment.

> Beloved, do not avenge yourselves, but rather give place to wrath; for it is written, "Vengeance is Mine, I will repay," says the Lord. (Rom. 12:19 NKJV)

> Then I saw another beast coming up out of the earth, and he had two horns like a lamb and spoke like a dragon. (Rev. 13:11 NKJV)

John saw another beast coming out of the earth. The beast had two horns like a lamb and spoke like a dragon. This term *lamb* here does not refer to Christ. The two horns refer to Jewish worship and religious authority. "Spoke as a dragon" means it gets its authority from the dragon. This beast performs signs to get people to worship the first beast, the Antichrist. He can call down fire from above and deceive people. He instructs the world to build an image of the Antichrist. The image has power, breathes, speaks; and this will cause many to believe in the Antichrist. He causes everyone to bear the mark on either his or her right hand or forehead. No one who doesn't have the mark will be able to buy or sell anything. The number of the beast is 666.

Revelation 14

Events in this chapter seem to be out of sync for chronological order. The events listed give reference to the things that are happening at different times in this book:

- The Lamb standing on Mount Zion with the 144,000. Christ is ready to return.
- The proclamations the three angels make. *First angel*: one last time to repent and fear God; the hour has come. *Second angel*: Babylon has fallen because of her sexual immorality with the world. *Third angel*: anyone who worships the beast and carries his mark; their torment is forever.
- The harvest of the Christians as Christ returns in all his glory. They are separated from the unbelieving.
- The grapes of wrath and the unbelieving take their stand with Satan. Christ defeats Satan at the battle of Armageddon.

John saw the Lamb and the 144,000 standing on Mount Zion. The 144,000 had the mark of their Father's name on their foreheads. Lamb is a reference to Christ. The 144,000 are the ones chosen from the twelve tribes of Israel. God's seal is on their forehead. Either Mount Zion is a reference to the early Jerusalem where the temple is or the heavenly Mount Zion. John heard voices, many waters and loud thunder, and playing of harps. They sing a new song before the throne, before the four living creatures and the elders. This song could be about the redemption and victory in Christ. They are the only ones able to learn this song, the ones in heaven, the redeemed from the earth, and the 144,000. The 144,000 are Jews; these are virgins. Virgins refer to the physical and spiritual purity. They follow the Lamb wherever He goes. They don't compromise with evil, and they reject false doctrine and refuse to take the mark of the beast. These 144,000 are God's special group of individuals being the first fruits to God and the Lamb. They have no deceit or fault in them. This refers to their testimony to Christ, and they reject the lie of the Antichrist. It implies that the harvest of Christians will continue, and many others will come to the saving faith of Jesus Christ.

John saw an angel, the first angel, having the everlasting gospel, and preached it to all the inhabitants of the earth. Every person will hear the message, which will fulfill the promise made in Matthew:

> And this gospel of the kingdom will be preached in all the world as a witness to all the nations, and then the end will come. (Matt. 24:14 NKJV)

We are to fear God and give glory to God. His judgment will come. We are to worship the one who made everything, God.

John saw another angel, the second angel. Babylon has fallen because she has deceived all the nations with her sexual immorality. Babylon is reference to being the harlot, the evil that man seeks after. The fall is when the light is removed from the world.

> The light of a lamp shall not shine in you anymore, and the voice of the bridegroom and the bride shall not be heard in you anymore. For your merchants were the great men of the earth, for by your sorcery all nations were deceived. (Rev. 18:23 NKJV)

John saw another angel, the third angel. Anyone who worships the beast, the image of the beast, and carries the mark of the beast will be tormented forever and ever. There will be no reprieve from this pain. The pain will not dull after time, no rest day or night in this place.

OVERVIEW OF REVELATION

> Here are the patience of the saints; here are those who keep the commandments of God and the faith of Jesus. (Rev. 14:12 NKJV)

Saints need to have patience while dealing with the end-time things that are happening around them. "Commandments of God" refer to the Jews. "Faith of Jesus" refers to the church.

> Then I heard a voice from heaven saying to me, "Write: 'Blessed are the dead who die in the Lord from now on.'" "Yes," says the Spirit, "that they may rest from their labors, and their works follow them." (Rev. 14:13 NKJV)

The second of the seven beatitudes listed in Revelation: "Blessed are the dead who die in the Lord form now on." "From now on" means from the time John is writing to his readers.

> There remains therefore a rest for the people of God. For he who has entered His rest has himself also ceased from his works as God did from His. (Heb. 4:9–10 NKJV)

John says,

> Then I looked, and behold, a white cloud, and on the cloud sat One like the Son of Man, having on His head a golden crown, and in His hand a sharp sickle. And another angel came out of the temple, crying with a loud voice to Him who sat on the cloud, "Thrust in Your sickle and reap, for the time has come, for You to reap, for the harvest of the earth is ripe." So He who sat on the cloud thrust in His sickle on the earth, and the earth was reaped. (Rev. 14:14–16 NKJV)

IS THERE TIME

Some think, where it says "the Son of Man," it is Christ. It says "One like the Son of Man." If this were Christ, why would it not say the Son of Man instead of One like the Son of Man? It says another angel. This makes me think the first one must be an angel. Why did another angel have to give direction and tell this one to thrust his sickle? Son of Man will command the angels, not the angels command Him. The golden crown would mean the one on the clouds would be reference to angelic being with authority. The harvest of Christians suggests, Christians are still on earth.

> And I looked, and behold, a white horse. He who sat on it had a bow; and a crown was given him, and he went out conquering and to conquer. (Rev. 6:2 NKJV)

The white horse in Revelation 6:2 is the Antichrist. Antichrist is trying to look like Christ here in 14:14. Satan is taking his best shot at the remaining population of believers. He is doing everything to put down anything relating to Christ or God. He wants the world to look at him as god.

> Then he opened his mouth in blasphemy against God, to blaspheme His name, His tabernacle, and those who dwell in heaven. It was granted to him to make war with the saints and to overcome them. And authority was given him over every tribe, tongue, and nation. All who dwell on the earth will worship him, whose names have not been written in the Book of Life of the Lamb slain from the foundation of the world. (Rev. 13:6–8 NKJV)

Another angel came out of the temple in heaven with a sharp sickle. Another angel came out of the altar, with power over fire. An angel thrust his sickle to the earth. An angel gathered the vine of the earth and threw the vine into the winepress of the wrath of God. The winepress of the wrath of God is a huge slaughter of life. The winepress trampled outside the city; the blood came out of the winepress.

Revelation 15

John returns to the second vision and picks up with what is happening just before the seven bowls, before the wrath of God in the world.

John saw another sign in heaven. There was seven angels having the seven plagues. He saw a sea of glass with fire, those having victory over the beast, the image of the beast, over his mark, and the number of his name. They sing the song of Moses and the song of the Lamb. It's interesting to note that they sing the song of Moses and the song of the Lamb. They are connecting the Old and the New Testament. Song of Moses would give reference to the Israelites deliverance from Egypt. Bondage they were under, and the care God gave them in the deliverance from Pharaoh's army. Song of the Lamb is reference to the redemptive power of the work of Christ in the life of His people. It shows the victory to the over comers on the other side. The smoke shows that God was going to act in judgment.

When the temple in heaven opened, out came seven angels having seven plagues. One of the four living creatures gave the seven angels seven bowls full of the wrath of God. Smoke filled the temple, and no one could enter until the seven plagues of the seven angels were complete.

Revelation 16

Then John heard a voice from the temple say to the seven angels, "Go and pour out your bowls of wrath of God on the earth" (Rev. 16:1b NKJV).

The First Bowl: The first angel went out and poured his bowl on the earth. There was terrible sores that fell upon anyone who had the mark of the beast, and anyone who worshiped the image of the beast. Reference to Revelation 16:2.

IS THERE TIME

The Egyptians faced something like this, but this is more severe.

> And it will become fine dust in all the land of Egypt, and it will cause boils that break out in sores on man and beast throughout all the land of Egypt. (Exod. 9:9 NKJV)

The Second Bowl: The second angel poured out his bowl on the sea. The sea became as blood. Everything that was living in the sea died. Reference to Revelation 16:3.

This is like the events that happen in the trumpets and to the Egyptians in Exodus. In the second trumpet, a third of the sea and its living creatures died, and in Egypt, the river became blood and the fish died.

> Then the second angel sounded: And something like a great mountain burning with fire was thrown into the sea, and a third of the sea became blood. And a third of the living creatures in the sea died, and a third of the ships were destroyed. (Rev. 8:8–9 NKJV)

The Egyptians had to face something like this in Exodus.

> Thus says the Lord: "By this you shall know that I am Lord. Behold, I will strike the water which are in the rivers with the rod that is in my hand, and they shall be turned to blood. And the fish that are in the river shall die, the river shall stink, and the Egyptians will loathe to drink the water of the river." (Exod. 7:17–18 NKJV)

The Third Bowl: The third angel poured out his bowl on the rivers and the springs. The waters of all the rivers and springs became blood. The angel of the waters praised God. The angel of the water was saying, "You are righteous, Lord. You are the One, who is—who was—and who is to be. You have judged all these things. For the blood of the saints and prophets have been shed. You gave them blood to drink for it was due them." Reference to Revelation 16:5–6.

The angel from the altar praised God, "Your judgments are true and righteous." In the trumpets, a third of the rivers and spring were affected. This is all the rivers and springs, and it made the water bitter.

The Fourth Bowl: The fourth angel poured out his bowl on the sun. He had power to scorch the people with fire and plagues. The people did not repent and they still blasphemed God. Reference to Revelation 16:8–9.

The Fifth Bowl: The fifth angel poured out his bowl on the throne of the beast and his kingdom. The people of the beast kingdom were in the dark and in pain and sores because of this bowl. They did not repent, and they still blasphemed God. Reference to Revelation 16:10–11.

The Sixth Bowl: The sixth angel poured out his bowl on the Euphrates River. The river dried up to prepare the way of the kings of the East. There were three unclean spirits like frogs coming out of the mouth of the dragon, beast, and false prophet. They were demons doing signs and going out to the kings of the earth to gather them to the great battle. The dragon, beast, and false prophet are an *unholy trinity*. Reference to Revelation 16:12–15.

Coming as a thief is the same warning given to the believers to be watchful because of Jesus unknown time for His return. We are to watch, wait, and be ready for our Lord's return.

> Behold, I am coming as a thief. Blessed is he who watches, and keeps his garments, least he walk naked and they see his shame. (Rev. 16:15 NKJV)

IS THERE TIME

> But as the days of Noah were, so also will the coming of the Son of Man be. (Matt. 24:37 NKJV)

> And did not know until the flood came and took them all away, so also will the coming of the Son of Man be. (Matt. 24:39 NKJV)

> Watch therefore, for you do not know what hour your Lord is coming. (Matt. 24:42 NKJV)

> Therefore you also be ready, for the Son of Man is coming at an hour you do not expect. (Matt. 24:44 NKJV)

The demons perform signs and gathered all the kings together at the place called Armageddon. Reference to Revelation 16:12–16.

The Seventh Bowl: The seventh angel poured out his bowl into the air. Then a loud voice from the throne, saying, "It is done!" This is the final act of judgment of the bowls, the last bowl before Christ comes. "There were noises, thundering, lightning, and a great earthquake." The earth has never seen an earthquake of this magnitude before. The great city fell and was divided into three parts. Babylon, the great harlot, is at the heart of the great earthquake and will extend to all the cities and nations of the earth. All the earth will feel the effect of this earthquake. God promised that the great Babylon would fall. Now the cup of His wrath is upon her. Every island and mountain on earth will fell the shake and destruction of this earthquake. Reference to Revelation 16:17–21.

Great hail from heaven falls and each weighting about a talent. A talent is approximately seventy-five pounds. To get an idea of the hail weighting seventy-five pounds: a man's bowling ball is about sixteen pounds, a thanksgiving turkey is between twenty to twenty-five pounds, and a bag of cement is sixty to ninety pounds. Hail of this size will be deadly, and there is destruction on a scale that the world has never seen before, truly devastating. Men did not repent, and they blasphemed God.

1 pound = 0.453592 kilograms/1 kilogram = 2.2 pounds

Revelation 17

John has a new vision, and this explains the harlot, the great Babylon. One of the seven angels who had the seven bowls told John to come. This angel will show John the judgment of the great harlot who sets on many waters. Many waters are reference to people, multitudes, and nations. The great harlot is Babylon. They seduced people with great power and wealth of the earth into committing adultery with Babylon. Their power, material possessions, false worship, and pride will consume them with whom the kings of the earth committed sexual immorality. The inhabitants of the earth were made drunk with the wine of her fornication. Reference to Revelation 17:1–2.

The woman in the wilderness is "Babylon, the mother of harlots." She is setting on a scarlet beast. Babylon is in league with the dragon and the beast pursing God's people. A scarlet beast relates to her or him as the beast of the sea, the Antichrist. The woman was dressed like a queen. Her golden cup was full of idolatry and unclean acts, sexual immorality that disgust God. God does not tolerate these immoral actions, and His justice will be for all who commit these atrocities.

> And on her forehead a name was written: MYSTERY, BABYLON THE GREAT, THE MOTHER OF HARLOTS AND OF THE ABOMINATIONS OF THE EARTH. (Rev. 17:5 NKJV)

Could the title of unclean acts in history somehow be the offspring of Babylon? They relate to the woman of nations being deceived by the serpent, the devil. The evil one is Babylon.

IS THERE TIME

> I saw the woman, drunk with the blood of the saints and with the blood of the martyrs of Jesus. And when I saw her, I marveled with great amazement. (Rev. 17:6 NKJV)

Being drunk with blood could mean a time of great slaughter. John was in position to watch the deception from afar. He knows of the great harlot and the evil that it spreads and the lives that evil destroys, and still, he marveled. This should be a *warning* to every believer in Christ. The deception will be great, and many will fall to the harlot. So watch and be ready, for the evil one will deceive as many as possible.

A person with spiritual understanding is receptive to God's truth. Babylon, she has wisdom but not God's truth in her mindset. "Seven heads" are the seven mountains that the woman sets on, which could be earthly kingdoms or empires. There are seven kings: five have fallen, one is, and the other one has not come yet. Five have fallen, it could be Egypt, Assyria, Babylon, Medo-Persia, and Greece. Most people think that one will be the Roman Empire. It could be the religious side of the Antichrist's monarchy. And when he comes, he must continue a short time. The mystery of the woman and the beast that carries her, who has seven heads and ten horns: the woman is the people of the earth that their name is not in the Book of Life. Reference to Revelation 17:9–11.

This empire could have authority in many nations, but be above the laws of those nations, and appear to be in touch with the masses. It couldn't be one person in authority, but rather a position that would have a successor. People in different nations would follow the empire over their nation, separate but affiliated with both and allegiance to the empire. What group or organization could exist with that kind of power and not claim to be an empire by name but act as an empire? Is this empire here now? This empire will be staying out of the controlling power of the world, only promoting peace for humanity and building creditability with the people of the world for when its time comes. The beast will be revived from a deadly wound, form an eighth empire out of the seventh. The eighth would be the one that the Antichrist would establish as a dictator with authority over the world.

Revelation 17:14 refers to the ten horns.

> These will make war with the Lamb, and the Lamb will overcome them, for He is Lord of lords and King of kings; and those who are with Him are called, chosen, and faithful. (Rev. 17:14 NKJV)

They are kings that have no kingdom but have authority for one hour. These have allegiance to the beast, which is the Antichrist. They rule alongside him and are like-minded with him. The Antichrist makes war with the Lamb. Christ is the Lamb and will overcome the Antichrist. He is Lord of lords and King of kings. Faithful and chosen are a reference to Gentile and Jewish believers in Christ. Jews are the chosen, and the church is the faithful. The harlot is the people and nations. They are the deceived of the world, the ones not written in the Book of Life. The beast's political aspect of Babylon will turn on the religious aspect of Babylon. The beast will hate the harlot. This satanic influence of Babylon has been in the world since the first sin.

Revelation 18

An angel from heaven came and, with a loud voice, said, "Babylon, the great, has fallen." It has become a place of demons and every foul spirit. They will be condemned to the bottomless pit. It is a prison for demons. This prison is a place of banishment. A prophecy, come out of her, that was proclaimed when Babylon was ready for judgment.

> My people, come out of the midst of her! And let everyone deliver himself from the fierce anger of the Lord. (Jer. 51:45 NKJV)

God will judge Babylon for her sinful works that she has committed over history. People need to remove themselves from participating and immersing themselves in the sinful act of Babylon's deception. If people stay immersed in the sin and follow her deception, they could receive some of her plagues. God will punish her for her iniquities and give her just as she gave. She will not like what God gives her. It will be double punishment for what she gave to the ones she deceived. In the manner that she glorified herself and lived luxuriously, she will be given torment and sorrow. Her attitude makes her think she is above God's control. Reference to Revelation 18:4–7.

The city will burn, and the Lord is strong and judges Babylon. People of the earth that made a profit from Babylon, they were looking from a distance and saw the smoke. They weep and mourn over her, for now no one buys and sells the things that made them rich. For in one hour, great riches became nothing.

> Rejoice over her, O heaven, and you holy apostles and prophets, for God has avenged you on her!
> (Rev. 18:20 NKJV)

Babylon is the symbol of all enemies of God and His people.

> The light of a lamp shall not shine in you anymore, and the voice of bridegroom and bride shall not be heard in you anymore. For your merchants were the great men of the earth, for by your sorcery all nations were deceived. And in her was found the blood of the prophets and the saints, and of all who were slain on the earth.
> (Rev. 18:23–24 NKJV)

"The light of a lamp," *Christians are the light.* The lamp is Christ.

> For you were once darkness, but now you are light in the Lord. Walk as Children of light...
> (Eph. 5:8 NKJV)

OVERVIEW OF REVELATION

He is telling us the rapture is about to happen. The light is God's word and His children. The bridegroom is Christ, and the bride is the church. This refers to all the saints, and saints killed and martyred throughout history. This answers what John was talking about when he quoted Jesus in John chapter 9 and 12.

> I must work the works of Him who sent Me while it is day; the night is coming when no one can work. (John 9:4 NKJV)

Then Jesus said to them,

> A little while longer the light is with you. Walk while you have the light, lest darkness overtake you; he who walks in darkness does not know where he is going. (John 12:35 NKJV)

> I have come as a light into the world, that whoever believes in Me should not abide in darkness. (John 12:46 NKJV)

Revelation 19

Rejoicing took place in heaven over the judgment of the great harlot. Everything about God's judgments is true and righteous. The harlot who corrupted the earth with her fornication will be no more. Many voices in heaven were saying,

> Alleluia! The Lord reigns. And I heard, as it were, the voice of a great multitude, as the sound of many waters and as the sound of mighty thunderings, saying, "Alleluia! For the Lord God Omnipotent reigns! Let us be glad and rejoice and give Him glory, for the marriage of the Lamb has come, and His wife has made herself ready." (Rev. 19:6–7 NKJV)

IS THERE TIME

The time has come for the marriage to the Lamb. Jesus is the bridegroom, and the bride is the church. The church is the chosen and the faithful, "the saints," who have made Him Lord and Savior.

Chosen and faithful all go through Jesus! "Jesus said to him, I am the way, the truth, and the life. No one comes to the Father except through Me" (John 14:6 NKJV). Then he said to me, "Write: 'Blessed are those who are called to the marriage supper of the Lamb!'" And he said to me, "These are true sayings of God" (Rev. 19:9 NKJV).

Christ returns on a white horse.

> Now I saw heaven opened, and behold, a white horse. And He who sat on him was called Faithful and True and in righteousness He judges and makes war. His eyes were like a flame of fire, and on His head many crowns. He had a name written that no one knew except Himself. He was clothed with a robe dipped in blood and His name is called The Word of God. And the armies in heaven, clothed in fine linen, white and clean, followed Him on white horses. Now out of the mouth goes a sharp sword, that with it He should strike the nations. And He Himself will rule them with a rod of iron. He Himself treads the winepress of the fierceness and wrath of Almighty God. And He has on His robe and on His thigh a name written KING OF KINGS AND LORD OF LORDS. (Rev. 19:11–16 NKJV)

John returns to the second vision. Christ returns, and this is His second coming. He returns on a white horse. He had a name that no one knew except Himself.

> He was clothed with a robe dipped in blood, and His name is called The Word of God. (Rev. 19:13 NKJV)

OVERVIEW OF REVELATION

There is such meaning in a name. The name that no one knew was revealed at Christ's second coming. Armies of heaven followed Him on white horses, and from His mouth, a sharp sword will strike the nations. The armies of Christ at His return are angels from heaven and the saints whom the grave holds (those who have fallen asleep). And the saints who are alive and enduring to the end, These saints will meet Him in the air. And He Himself will rule them with a rod of iron.

> And He has on His robe and on His thigh a name written: KING OF KINGS AND LORD OF LORDS. (Rev. 19:16 NKJV)

At Christ's second coming, Christ will return with the trumpet of God, then the believers in Christ will be raptured up to be with him forever. Paul told the Thessalonians,

> For the Lord Himself will descend from heaven with a shout, with the voice of an archangel, and with the trumpet of God. And the dead in Christ will rise first. Then we who are alive and remain shall be caught up together with them in the clouds to meet the Lord in the air. And thus we shall always be with the Lord. Therefore comfort one another with these words. (1 Thess. 4:16–18 NKJV)

The rapture happens as Jesus is returning: the dead in Christ first, then we who are left will join Him in the air, caught up (rapture) at the trumpet of God.

John saw an angel, and the angel said to the birds with a loud voice, "Come and prepare. The birds shall eat; flesh of kings, flesh of captains, flesh of mighty men, and flesh of horses and those who sat on them. The birds shall eat on the armies of the ones who oppose Christ."

Then John saw the beast and his armies come together to make war on Christ and His army. Then the beast and the false prophet are captured and thrown into the lake of fire. This is the eternal destiny of all who don't believe in the saving power of Christ. The sword that came out of the mouth of Christ killed the rest of the beast army.

Revelation 20

Next, John saw an angel coming down from heaven having the keys to the bottomless pit and has a chain in his hand. He took the dragon, serpent of old (which is the devil, Satan), and bound him and cast him into the bottomless pit for a thousand years. He deceives no one anymore during the thousand years. After the thousand years, Satan is released for a time.

At the last fall of Babylon and the return of Christ. The church is raptured out to be with Christ. The bride is the church and is now with Christ. Believers will have a part with Christ during the rule of the millennial.

> Do you not know that the saints will judge the world? And if the world will be judged by you, are you unworthy to judge the smallest matters? Do you know we shall judge angels? How much more, things that pertain to this life? If then you have judgments concerning things pertaining to this life, do you appoint those who are least esteemed by the church to judge? (1 Cor. 6:2–4 NKJV)

Paul was telling the people of Corinth that one day they would judge the unbelievers and angels. They should be able to take care of problems between themselves rather than the pagan courts. In the millennial kingdom, Jesus will set up authority for saints and authority is transferred from angels to men.

OVERVIEW OF REVELATION

> For He has not put the world to come, of which we speak, in subjection to angels. (Heb. 2:5 NKJV)

The overcoming saints will rule together with Christ in His kingdom. Christ will reign for one thousand years. John saw thrones and saints sat on them, and judgment was committed to them. John saw the souls of those who had been beheaded for their witness to Jesus and for the word of God. They are the ones who had not worshiped the beast or his image, and the one who didn't receive the beast's marks on their foreheads or their hands. They lived and reigned with Christ for a thousand years. Reference to Revelation 20:4.

The church raptured out of this world to be with Christ when He returns at the last trumpet. Our final victory will be in that instance.

> In the moment, in the twinkling of an eye, at the last trumpet. For the trumpet will sound, and the dead will be raised incorruptible, and we shall be changed. For this corruptible must put on incorruption, and this mortal must put on immortality. (1 Cor. 15:52–53 NKJV)

Some think that this put the rapture at the last of the seven trumpets, before the seven bowls. The last trumpet is when Christ returns, not between the judgments of the trumpets and the bowls. In chapter 13 of Mark, it talks about when the end will happen: verses 1–2 is the destruction of the temple, verses 3 to 8 is the signs of the times, verses 9 to 23 is the end of age/ the great tribulation, verses 24 to 27 is the coming of the Son of Man. Mark says in 13:24, "But in those days, after the tribulation." Mark says in 3:26, "Then they will see the Son of Man coming in the clouds with great power and glory."

The Father will judge the Jews and the Gentiles, the believers and the unbelievers. All will be judged. There are two resurrections: all the people will be judged in either the first or second resurrection. If you are a part of the first resurrection, you will not be a part of the second.

IS THERE TIME

Jesus is speaking to John:

> Do not marvel at this; for the hour is coming in which all who are in the grave will hear His voice and come forth-those who have done good, to the resurrection of life, and those who have done evil, to the resurrection of condemnation. (John 5:28–29 NKJV)

The first resurrection will be the resurrection of life, believers in Christ. The second will be the resurrection of evil, the unbelievers in Christ. They will go before the great white throne of judgment.

> Blessed and holy is he who has part in the first resurrection. Over such the second death has no power, but they shall be priest of God and of Christ, and shall reign with Him a thousand years. (Rev. 20:6 NKJV)

At the beginning of the thousand years, the Christians have already been raptured and are with Christ. Satan has been put in prison, not to influence anyone for a thousand years. There are people who don't believe in Christ and didn't believe in Satan's authority either. They were just getting by. Now for a thousand years, they will experience life without the influence of Satan's lies on this world. These people will live their lives with only seeing Jesus influence.

Now the thousand years have ended, and Satan is released from his prison. Satan will go out to the four corners of the earth to gather anyone that has not believed in Christ to make war. They surrounded the camps of the Saints and the beloved city. Fire came down from heaven and devoured them. Satan is placed into the lake of fire, where the beast and the false prophet are. The torment will go on day and night, forever and ever, *with no relief.*

The second resurrection time is now before the great white throne judgments. Now all the dead are standing before God, and the books are opened. The books are a record of works done in this life. "For all have sinned and fall short of the glory of God" (Rom. 3:23 NKJV).

God's grace will save many. They received this grace by faith in Jesus Christ. "For by grace you have been saved through faith, and that not of yourselves; it is the gift of God" (Eph. 2:8 NKJV).

No one will be judged acceptable by his works. "Not of works, lest anyone should boast" (Eph. 2:9 NKJV).

John saw another book opened, the Book of Life. The dead judged according to what is in the book.

> The sea gave up the dead who were in it, and the Dead and Hades delivered up the dead who were in them. And they were judged, each one according to his works. Then Death and Hades were cast into the lake of fire. This is the second death. And anyone not found written in the Book of Life was cast into the lake of fire. (Rev. 20:13–15 NKJV)

Revelation 21

There is a new heaven and a new earth, the old have passed away. We will have a new body; we will be a new creation. Reference to 2 Corinthians 5:17. The New Jerusalem was coming down out of heaven. The believers shall be His people, and God will be with His people. God will dwell with them, as did Christ. All things will be a new creation. There is a new heaven, earth, and men.

> And God will wipe away every tear from their eyes; there shall be no more death, nor sorrow, nor crying. There shall be no more pain, for the former things have passed away. (Rev. 21:4 NKJV)

There was one on the throne. He is the Alpha and the Omega. He is the true and faithful God. The one who sat on the throne will make all things new. John was instructed to write these words that are true and faithful. God told John it was done! "I am the first and the

IS THERE TIME

last, the beginning and the end. I will give water of life to everyone who thirsts. The ones who overcome will inherit all things, and I will be his God, and he shall be my son." Reference to Revelation 21:7.

People need to wake up and realize the decisions they make now on how they speak, act, and treat others can have very harsh consequences on their eternal life, whether they will be in heaven or hell. Compare Revelation 21:8 to 1 Corinthians 6:9–10.

> But cowardly, unbelieving, abominable, murderers, sexually immoral, sorcerers, idolaters, and all liars shall have their part in the lake of fire and brimstone, which is the second death. (Rev. 21:8 NKJV)

> Do you not know that the unrighteous will not inherit the kingdom of God? Do not be deceived. Neither fornicators, nor idolaters, nor adulterers, nor homosexuals, nor sodomites, nor thieves, nor covetous, nor drunkards nor revilers, nor extortions, will inherit the kingdom of God. (1 Cor. 6:9–10 NKJV)

John saw the great city, the holy Jerusalem, descending from heaven. Jerusalem had a high wall with twelve gates, three on each of the four walls. Each gate had angels and names of one the twelve tribes of Israel. They also had twelve foundations, and the names were the twelve apostles of Christ. Reference to Revelation 21:12–14.

At each gate was a Pearl. Christ is the Pearl of Great Peace. Jesus Christ is our way to God, the only way to God, the only way to the Father. There will be no admittance into the city without a personal relationship with Jesus Christ. Just knowing about Jesus is not enough. Even believing that Christ was a good and mighty person as He walked on earth many years ago not enough. Having knowledge of Christ is not enough. Even believing that there is a Christ is not enough. It takes more than knowing; it takes having Christ as your personal Savior, knowing and believing that Christ is God's Son, and a personal relationship with Jesus Christ for admittance.

I have always found it interesting that the foundation would be with the church, not the tribes of Israel. The gates are the tribes of Israel, and the foundation of the New Jerusalem is the church. Think how important the foundation is in any structure. No structure can stand without a strong foundation. The doors are very important, the way into the city. But the foundation is what the city is built on, and supports it, and binds it together. The strength is in the foundation of any structure. We should never minimize our part in the scheme of the New Jerusalem. How much faith and trust does God put in the church to make the church the foundation of the New Jerusalem? This speaks to how important God takes our adoption into His family. Because of Christ, we are part of the family of God. We partake of the promise that God made to Abraham and Jacob. Christians, saints, the church is adopted into a very special family, God's family. Our God is an awesome God. Amen!

> The foundation of the walls of the city were adorned with all kinds of precious stones: the first foundation was jasper, the second sapphire, the third chalcedony, the fourth emerald, the fifth sardonyx, the sixth sardius, the seventh chrysolite, eighth beryl, the ninth topaz, the tenth chrysoprase, eleventh jacinth, and the twelfth amethyst. (Rev. 21:19–20 NKJV)

A resemblance of colors, the stones and gems of the walls that are the foundation of the colors that make up the rainbow:

The Colors of the Foundation		The Colors of the Rainbow
jasper	blackish green	red
sapphire	Purplish blue	orange

chalcedony	translucent various colors	yellow
emerald	rich green	green
saedius	red	blue
sardonyx	reddish brown	deep reddish blue
chrysolite	greenish	violet reddish blue
beryl	various: green, blue, yellow, pink	
topaz	transparent brownish yellow	
chrysoprasus	golden green	
jacinth	orange	
amethyst	purple or bluish violet	

The light that shines on creation will no longer need to exist: the sun, moon, and stars. Christ is light. The glory of God will light everything. The names that are written in the Lamb's Book of Life are the only ones who can enter the gates in the walls of the New Jerusalem. Sin will not abide there. Everything of evil has been thrown into the Lake of Fire, never to be seen again.

Revelation 22

There is a river of running water coming out of the throne of God and the Lamb. This river is crystal clear, and nothing will pollute it. The river is in the middle of the street running down both sides of the tree of life. The tree of life will have twelve fruits, and each one bears its fruit every month. Its leaves are for healing the nations. There will be no curse in this city, for the throne of God and the Lamb will be in it, and His servants will serve Him. They shall see His face, and His name shall be on their foreheads. There will be no outside light. The Lord is light and will provide their light. The inhabitants of the New Jerusalem shall live and reign forever and ever.

OVERVIEW OF REVELATION

The conclusion to all of John's visions, the time is near, is meant to wake people up. People become numb to the things that are going on all around us. It seems we have eyes but do not see. We have ears, but don't hear the truths of God. The master of deception will deceive us unless we are very careful. We will believe his lies. These visions inform the true believers. These things will take place soon. Jesus is speaking in 22:7.

> Behold, I am coming quickly! Blessed is he who keeps the words of this prophecy of this book. (Rev. 22:7 NKJV)

John, for the second time, fell down and worshiped the angel, and the angel told John,

> "Don't worship me, worship God." Then he said to me, "See that you do not do that. For I am your fellow servant, and of your brethren and prophets, and of those who keep the words of this book. Worship God." (Rev. 22:9 NKJV)

This shows how weak and easily convinced we can become, John worshiping wrong because of what he saw. The deception will be great and will come at us from all different directions. We need to be vigilant and keep our guard up. Everyone needs to stay focused and keep our eyes on the Lord, not the world. The world will paint a very convincing way of telling Satan's lies, not God's truths.

Don't hide what you have heard. Tell everyone. Jesus tells the churches He is coming quickly, and His reward is with Him. He is the first and the last, the Alpha and the Omega. Blessed are the ones who do His commandments; they are the ones having the right to enter the gates. No other will be able to enter the gates of the New Jerusalem. Jesus tells the churches that He is the offspring of David and the bright and morning star. The spirit and the bride say, "Come!"

IS THERE TIME

A warning to anyone who adds or takes away from this book: anyone who adds to the book, God will add plagues to him. Anyone who takes away for this book, God will take away his part from the Book of Life.

The book ends with these words:

> He who testifies to these things says, Surely I am coming quickly. Amen. Even so, come, Lord Jesus! The grace of our Lord Jesus Christ be with you all. Amen. (Rev. 22:20–21 NKJV)

The sacrifice and persecution that Christians will go through are but a passing of time. The reward is great, but the alternative is devastating: separation from God. Think of being in a place that has no input of good, no one that is looking out for you, just pain and suffering. Being eternally with Satan and never being able to see or feel the presence of God. Now that is a definition of hell!

Hell is a very real place, a place of final separation
from God of which there is no return!
Heaven is a very real place, a place never separated from God!
Amen!

CHAPTER 14

The Generation When Israel Becomes a Nation

THE PARABLE OF THE FIG tree is important. The verses in Matthew and Mark are almost word for word. Luke says it a little differently but gets the same point across. These verses are telling us the generation that sees the return of Israel to their homeland, and restored to a nation, will be the beginning of the Laodicean church age. The parable of the fig tree is in Matthew, Mark, and Luke.

Matthew:

> Now learn this parable from the fig tree: When its branch has already become tender and puts forth leaves, you know that summer is near. So you also, when you see all these things, know that it is near-at the doors! Assuredly, I say to you, this generation will by no means pass away till all these things take place. Heaven and earth will pass away, but My words will by no means pass away. (Matt. 24:32–35 NKJV)

IS THERE TIME

Mark:

> Now learn this parable from the fig tree: When its branch has already become tender, and puts forth leaves, you know that summer is near. So you also, when you see all these things happening, know that it is near-at the doors! Assuredly, I say to you, this generation will by no means pass away till all these things take place. Heaven and earth will pass away, but My words will by no means pass away. (Mark 13:28–31 NKJV)

Luke:

> Then He spoke to them a parable: Look at the fig tree, and all the trees. When they are already budding, you see and know for yourselves that summer is near. So you also, when you see all these things happening, know that the kingdom of God is near. Assuredly, I say to you, this generation will by no means pass away till all things take place. Heaven and earth will pass away, but My words will by no means pass away. (Luke 21:29–33 NKJV)

In Matthew and Mark, it starts with the words "Now learn this." This is one of those phrases that should grab you attention. *Important, important.* "This generation will not pass away until these things take place." We should be ready for when things take place. Things will move quickly. Don't be caught sleeping. *Wake up*!

The fig tree is symbolic of Israel. The "branch becomes tender" is Israel when it becomes a nation restored. "Puts forth leaves" would be the land becomes fruitful and has plenty. "Summer is near," Christ's return is near. "When you see all these things happening," they are signs of the end time. The end of the church age will approach us and be hard to see for the ones who are not looking. Watch out for the people who claim to be Christ. There will be nations and kingdoms against each other. There will be wars and rumors of wars. The earth will have famine, pestilence, and earthquakes.

Many will claim to be Christ and show signs. Christ has warned us that many false Christs would come. His word to us is watch for these signs. Get ready. Christ is about to open the door of heaven. "This generation will not pass away until all these things take place," the coming of the Son of Man and the sign will be the appearing of Him in the heavens. All the unbelieving tribes of Christ on the earth will morn. They will see the Son of Man (Christ) coming in the clouds of heaven. He will have with Him great power and glory.

"Heaven and earth will pass away, but My words will by no means pass away." Many things will cease to exist, but His word will never go away. We need to be ready and be about doing the Father's work until the end, when Christ returns. Christ will return in the hour that you least expect.

In the last days, things will happen, and signs will appear. Will you be able see what is happening around you? Will you accept the lie but not see the truth? Do we know the signs to look for? How do you think governments will look at Christians during the coming times? Think about what is available now, what is in everyday use that Satan can use, that we take for granted?

Vehicles have systems that track your position. This system is in every vehicle that we purchase. Whether you activate it or not, it is in the vehicles we drive today. I think it's been there for several years. If the vehicle is stolen, the police can find the vehicle. They can track it. It will make it possible if someone wants to find you. They will know right where your vehicle is at. This is in the name of safety and helping you. The Antichrist will know where your vehicle is at all the time you are in your vehicle. If you lock your keys in your vehicle, they can unlock it for you from miles away. This is all in the name of your safety and helping you. If the Antichrist doesn't want you to get into your vehicle for whatever reason, he can lock you out of your vehicle. If the he doesn't want you to get out of your vehicle, he can lock you in it.

IS THERE TIME

In the name of security, people could have their personal, health, and banking information implanted in the back of their hand or forehead for ease of use. For your safety, you will not have any fear of losing it. With so much identity thief going on in the world, your identity will finally be safe. You can make all your purchases by just scanning your hand or forehead. This will all be in the name of making you safer. The chip will make it possible to track you for your safety if needed. No more lost or stolen cards. You never will lose it. In the end times, the Antichrist will be able to find you. Remember the mark of the beast. Do not take it, and do not be deceived.

Most people are getting to feel more at ease with the new technologies of communication, even the marks on their bodies. We have a law that you must use a hands-free cell phone while you are driving, which makes the user safer. This device makes it easy to stay in touch. People are getting so use to them; they leave them in their ear almost all the time. In the fifties, they used subliminal messages in films to get people to buy when they weren't planning on purchasing anything. Wonder what they can do now with all the advances in technologies. If you leave a cell phone attached to your ear all day, what kind of mind games or control are they capable of doing. As before, we will not know until it is too late, if we know at all.

All television signals have to be digital, better quality, picture clarity—one more way to influence people and control what they think, say, and do. A lot of knowledge in humans comes through what we see. Our eyes open our minds too many influences and control if we are not careful. We need to guard our minds. Remember, the signal is coming into your house, one that a computer controls. But who controls the computer? Most people are addicted to the entertainment brought into their homes and never give it a second thought. Have you ever noticed that when you search for something on the net, the next day there is an advertisement to buy it? We are being monitored in our daily life; people just don't recognize it. Such an enjoyable entertainment. It is right there so easy to access. Have you ever wondered why, with all those choices and channels, why is so hard to find something to watch. I catch myself flipping the channels looking for something to watch. All of sudden I realize, I have been at this channel twice already. Addiction can take many forms. It does not have to be drugs or alcohol.

One of the steps for the Antichrist is one-world banking. They will standardize the banking and currency in the name of making it safer and easier for people of the world to do business. Another step for the Antichrist is government-controlled health care, in the name of caring for the poor.

I have always wondered who would be the Antichrist police force. Who would buy into that way of thinking? Will they be about peace, justice, right and wrong? They will be about forcing their brand of justice on everyone. Their way of justice will be about hate, evil, and having nothing to do with peace and justice or right and wrong for all. The radical terrorists believe with their whole heart and mind that if you don't believe the way they do, you should be stopped or killed. They believe it is their right, duty, and obligation to make that happen.

Each Christian needs to be about our Father's business. We are to share Christ with a lost world, no matter what the popular opinion is. Christ is near, and His return is very near and it is getting closer with each passing day.

All this convenience in the world, but at what cost? Signs of the times are everywhere and more seem to appear every day. How far away do you think the last days will be? No one knows but the Father. The one thing we all know is we are to be ready. The last days will be sooner than most people think, they are approaching. They will be here before you know it. You will be caught sleeping if you don't keep watch. His word reminds us several times: *keep watch*. You need to keep watch, or one day you will see what's going on and say, "Why didn't I see what was going on around me." We need to look for the signs. They are all around us. The Bible tells all of us what we need to know. The signs are all listed in the Bible for us to see. His word reveals the signs to us if we but read it. My suggestion to you is to open the Bible and read it *daily*.

IS THERE TIME

We are in the final days!
Will you be ready for His return?

Answer to the question:
Is there time?
Yes!

You can accept Christ any time before His return
Sooner would be better than latter

Answer to the question:
Is there time?
No!
Because
There is no guarantee of tomorrow

When Christ returns it is too late,
At that time the decision you have made is final!
And that decision is for eternity!

You will either be in
Heaven or hell

Both are very real places

CHAPTER 15

Do You Know?

Do you know Christ? Do you only know about Him? There is a difference. There needs to be a personal relationship with Christ. To know Christ is not a group experience, I repeat, not a group experience. Not that you cannot accept Christ in a large gathering of people. However, to know Christ is a personal experience between you and Christ.

If you know about Christ and would like to know Him personally, then read this chapter. Before you start, get to a place where you can spend a few minutes alone in a quiet place, with no interruptions. Clear your mind of the everyday happenings. Look for the truth, God's truth, and what it means to you.

God loves everyone and wants no one left behind.

> For God so loved the world that He gave his only begotten Son, that whoever believes in Him should not perish but have everlasting life. (John 3:16 NKJV)

Everyone will live forever in God's presence or separated from Him forever. God has a plan for every person, and that is to have a full and meaningful life. God's love was so great for us that He gave His Son to die on a cross for you and me.

> The thief does not come except to steal, and to kill, and to destroy. I have come that they may have life, and that they may have it more abundantly. (John 10:10 NKJV)

The introduction of sin into the relationship between God and man is when Adam and Eve chose to disobey God. God's word calls this sin. All men and women are from Adam and Eve and born with a sin nature. This is a direct result of the sin that they introduced, which separates man from God.

> For the wages of sin is death, but the gift of God is eternal life in Christ Jesus our Lord. (Rom. 6:23 NKJV)

God created man to have fellowship with Him. Man cannot span the gulf of sin between man and God. There is only one way to bridge this separation, and that is Jesus Christ. Christ paid the price for my sin, your sin, and everyone's sin. Jesus Christ was the payment for all sin. Christ was the only man to live without sin, born of a virgin, God's Son. He gave His life to pay the price for a lost world. He took our place on the cross. God showed His love for each of us by taking our place on the cross.

> But God demonstrates His love towards us, in that while we were still sinners, Christ died for us. (Rom. 5:8 NKJV)

Jesus Christ died on the cross. They buried him in a tomb. He rose on the third day. The grave could not hold Him. He lives today.

> For I delivered to you first of all that which I also received: that Christ died for our sins accord-

> ing to the Scriptures, and that He was buried, and that He rose the third day according to the Scriptures, and that He was seen by Cephas, then by the twelve. After that He was seen by over five hundred brethren at once, of whom the greater part remain to the present, but some have fallen asleep. (1 Cor. 15:3–6 NKJV)

Jesus Christ is the only way to reach God.

> Jesus said to him, I am the way, the truth, and the life. No one comes to the Father except through Me. (John 14:6 NKJV)

It is not enough to know these things. You must accept and personally receive him as your Lord and Savior. And he brought them out and said, "Sirs, what must I do to be saved?" So they said, "Believe on the Lord Jesus Christ, and you will be saved…" (Acts 16:30–31 NKJV).

Salvation is a gift from God, free.

> For by grace you have been saved through faith, and that not of yourselves; it is the gift of God, not of works, lest anyone should boast. (Eph. 2:8–9 NKJV)

With a personal invitation, Christ will come into your life.

> Behold, I stand at the door and knock. If anyone hears My voice and opens the door, I will come in to him and dine with him, and he with Me. (Rev. 3:20 NKJV)

IS THERE TIME

When you turn from self to God and confess your sins and believe that Christ will forgive your sins, that is repentance. You will receive Christ by faith.

> That if you confess with your mouth the Lord Jesus and believe in your heart that God has raised Him from the dead, you will be saved. For with the heart one believes unto righteousness, and with the mouth confession is made unto salvation. (Rom. 10:9–13 NKJV)
>
> You can receive Christ by *praying*. Prayer is nothing more than *talking* to God.
>
> All who receive Christ will have eternal life the very moment you invite Christ into your life. (1 John 5:11–13)

The moment you receive Christ by faith:

Christ comes into your life	Revelation 3:20; Colossians 1:27
Your sins are forgiven	Colossians 1:14
You became a child of God	John 1:12
You receive eternal life	John 5:24

God created you for a specific reason and purpose (John 10:10; 2 Cor. 5:17; 1 Thess. 5:16–18)

DO YOU KNOW?

We live by faith (Gal. 3:11).

How? You must trust in God with more and more, with everything in your life. To enjoy Christ's love to the fullest, we need to grow. The list below is how growth happens.

G	*G*o to God in prayer *daily*.	John 15:7
R	*R*ead God's word *daily*.	Acts 17:11
O	*O*bey God *daily*.	John 14:21
W	*W*itness for Christ *daily*.	Matthew 4:19
T	*T*rust God for everything *daily*.	1 Peter 5:7
H	*H*oly Spirit: allowing Him to control and empower your *daily* life.	Acts 1:8; Galatians 5:16–18, 25–26

You will notice, in the list of how growth happens, is the word *daily*. This is not every other day, once a week, monthly, or quarterly. It is involving Him *daily* in every aspect of your life.

Important   *Important*   *Important*

Get involved and fellowship with other Christians in a good Bible preaching church.

Important   *Important*   *Important*

> And let us consider one another in order to stir up love and good works, not forsaking the assembling of ourselves together, as is the manner of some, but exhorting one another, and so much the more as you see the Day approaching. (Heb. 10:24–25 NKJV)

"Not forsaking the assembling of ourselves together." It is so important that we meet together to build each other up. We need to strength each other, not tear each other down. Leave the tearing down to the world. We don't need to help them in that.

IS THERE TIME

Study to shew thyself approved unto God, a workman that needeth not to be ashamed, rightly dividing the word of truth. (2 Tim. 2:15 KJV)

Keep God's word present in your mind.

Always study His word, so you will know what you hear men say is what God has said!
May God be with you in all that you do and say!
God bless you in your journey with Christ.

Remember:

Therefore, to him who knows to do good and does not do it, to him it is sin. (James 4:17 NKJV)

ABOUT THE AUTHOR

THE AUTHOR WAS SAVED AT an earlier age, junior high. The book of Revelation has fascinated him—the end times, and how does it all fit together? The common detonator is the Trinity: God the Father, God the Son, and God the Holy Spirit. They are three in one, but each one has their purpose. The author feels that this book is God working through him. He had been working on this book for several  years, around 2004. In his prayer time, back in 2004, in the morning before he headed for work, he felt the Lord telling him something. The more he prayed about it, the stronger he felt the Lord was telling him to write a book. He didn't think about it, prayed for direction, nothing. Just said no.

He argued with the Lord. Who would want to read anything he had to say? He worked with his hands for a living, a mechanic. After all, English was his worst subject in school. Spelling was the worst. Punctuation was just as bad. His talks with the Lord, his morning prayer time, were not good. Understand, his prayer time has always been the joy of his life. It is where he gets his peace, his calm from. And now he told the Lord, no. For the first time, he felt he was having a disconnect trying to talk to the Lord. One of his greatest joys was not there. He would pray, and instead of being engulfed with peace as before, there was a wall. This went on for a few months. He didn't like his prayer time anymore. He wanted his joy back.

He surrender to what the Lord wanted him to do, but he kind of hung on to a little of his attitude. He told the Lord, "Okay, I will do it. Lord, you know nobody will want to read anything I write. I have no talent, no experience in writing a book. I am the wrong person for this task." The problem now was that he surrendered to write the book, just not his all. The next morning when he went to prayer, something happened. He felt the Lord telling him He would show him. The Lord told him that he had written for years a fictional story, finish it and he will publish it. Now he has heard how hard it was to publish a book. He thought, *Well, that takes care of that.* It was almost impossible to get a book published, especially for someone like him. He has never considered that writing for stress could become a book. But he did enjoy writing.

He finished that book and submitted it to a publisher. He knew nothing was going to happen for someone who cannot spell or punctuate. His attitude changed when he received the response from the publisher. When he read the response, the only thing that came to his mind was, "O ye of little faith!" The Lord can make anything happen. He went to prayer right then. He apologizes, asked for forgiveness of a cold heart and depending on self instead of the Lord. From that moment on, he worked on the book with a new attitude and drive. He looked back on all that had transpired about this book and thought, *Who in their right mind says no to the Lord?* And to make matters worse, who argues with the Lord and expects to win the argument? When he surrendered with the right attitude, guess what came back? His joy. Praise the Lord, his joy was back, and there was his peace and calm.

The book didn't sell well but was published as the Lord said it would be. He is correcting that book now. His hope and prayer is that this book will cause people to open their Bibles and read them and study them. If you read this book with an open mind and a prayerful humble attitude, you will realize that God's word is in it. The author knows the reader will be blessed. The book shows the Old Testament and the New Testament. It shows the seventy weeks of Daniel as they fit together. It also shows the church age, sexually immoral, and the rapture, and how they fit together. He knows the Lord will inspire and bless the reader of this book.

God bless and enjoy your travel with the Lord as he leads your path.

Printed in the USA
CPSIA information can be obtained
at www.ICGtesting.com
JSHW081908191123
52095JS00001B/63

We live in a culture where there is no time for ourselves. We need to slow down and make time for ourselves. Make time for the Lord. Everybody is self-sufficient in everything these days. We need to have the right attitude in our service to the Lord. God's strategy for successful living character is more important than intelligence. The Bible is God's word to man, not man's word about God. God's word reveals the purpose and plan for man.

Satan is conditioning us for what he is bringing in the future, to make it look acceptable. God meant for sex to build a bond between a man and a woman in marriage, but man can pervert anything. Sex is one of the most powerful things humans have to deal with.

The seventy weeks of Daniel: the cross is at the end of the sixty-two weeks, the cross is at the beginning of the seven weeks, and the cross is in the middle of the final week. The cross is what ties this prophecy together.

The church age was put into place to reach the lost. Christ had five things to say about each of the seven church ages: description, commendation, criticism, instruction, and promises.

Before Christ is the Tribulation period. After Christ is the End-Time Tribulation period. The Great Tribulation starts with the trumpets and goes until the return of Christ. The purpose of the Bible is to reveal Jesus Christ as the Messiah.

Heaven and hell are real places. With one, we will always be with God, and with the other, we will always be separated from God. Both will be forever.

$18.95

ISBN 979-8-88943-136-7